Songs of Spiritual Experience

Songs of
Spiritual Experience

Tibetan Buddhist Poems of
Insight and Awakening

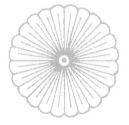

Selected and translated by
Thupten Jinpa and Jaś Elsner

SHAMBHALA
Boston & London
2000

SHAMBHALA PUBLICATIONS, INC.

HORTICULTURAL HALL

300 MASSACHUSETTS AVENUE

BOSTON, MASSACHUSETTS 02115

www.shambhala.com

9 8 7 6 5 4 3 2 1

First Edition

Printed in the United States of America

⊗ This edition is printed on acid-free paper that meets
the American National Standards Institute Z39.48 Standard.
Distributed in the United States by Random House, Inc.,
and in Canada by Random House of Canada Ltd

Library of Congress Cataloging-in-Publication Data
Songs of spiritual experience: Tibetan Buddhist poems of insight and awakening/
selected and translated by Thupten Jinpa and Ja's Elsner
p.   cm.
Includes bibliographical references.
ISBN 1-57062-550-6
I. Thupten Jinpa.   II. Elsner, Ja's.
PL3717.S64   2000
895'.410080382—dc21   00-041990

CONTENTS

Foreword   xi

Preface   xiii

Translators' Introduction   1

EVOCATIONS OF LIFE'S TRANSIENCE

from Tunes on the Absence of Elaborations   31
  Za Paltrül Rinpoche

A Meditation on Impermanence   33
  Gungthang Tenpai Drönme

Movements of Dancing Lightning   38
  Chone Lama Rinpoche

A Word-Brush Drawing of the Monster-Form of
Impermanence on Mind's Stone Tablet   42
  Chone Lama Rinpoche

Inspire Me to Remember Death   46
  Kelsang Gyatso, seventh Dalai Lama

Ramblings of an Aged Man   51
  Gungthang Tenpai Drönme

YEARNING FOR SOLITUDE

The Red Rocky Mountain   63
  Milarepa

The Joys of the Solitary Hills   64
  Kalden Gyatso

A Song by a Yogi in Solitude   66
Shapkar Tsogdruk Rangdröl

Longing for the Mountains of Solitude   68
Za Paltrül Rinpoche

CALLING THE GURU FROM AFAR

A Beggar and His Guru   73
Milarepa

May I See My Guru Again and Again   75
Natsok Rangdröl

A Song of Desolation   77
Kalden Gyatso

On the Death of Kyabje Trijhang Rinpoche, 1982   78
Zemey Lobsang Palden

ECHOES OF EMPTINESS

Reflections on Emptiness   83
Tsongkhapa

In Praise of the Vision of Father Lobsang   85
Kelsang Gyatso, seventh Dalai Lama

Ramblings of a Drunken Bee   87
Chone Lama Rinpoche

A Response to a Logician   91
Milarepa

A Spontaneous Song Evoked by the Dream-Girl   93
Chone Lama Rinpoche

A Sky with a Center and Borders!   96
Longchen Rabjampa

Melodies of an Echo   100
    Chone Lama Rinpoche

The Love Dance of Emptiness and Appearance   102
    Chone Lama Rinpoche

Awake from the Slumber of Ignorance!   105
    Kelsang Gyatso, seventh Dalai Lama

Recognizing My Mother   109
    Changkya Rölpai Dorje

STEPS ON THE PATH TO AWAKENING

An Experiential Tune on Eight Dream Practices   117
    Drakpa Gyaltsen

Lines of Self-Encouragement Written in Lhasa
in the Year of the Horse   119
    Rangjung Dorje, third Karmapa

Wielding a Club in the Darkness   121
    Tsangpa Gyare

A Song of Self-Encouragement toward True
Renunciation   123
    Chone Lama Rinpoche

Laying the Ground for Forbearance   125
    Rangjung Dorje, third Karmapa

On How to Engage in a Meditative Path   127
    Drakpa Gyaltsen

A Prayer for the Flourishing of Virtues   129
    Tsongkhapa

VISIONS OF MYSTIC CONSCIOUSNESS

A Taste of Meditation   137
Tsangpa Gyare

The Dakinis' Feast   139
Natsok Rangdröl

An Adamantine Song on Purposeless Pursuits   140
Longchen Rabjampa

A Dance of Unwavering Devotion   144
Chone Lama Rinpoche

A Song on the View of Voidness   147
Karma Trinley

On How to Apply the Antidotes   151
Drakpa Gyaltsen

Cutting the Rope of Conceit   153
Machik Labdrön

A Feast Song in Lhasa   155
Rangjung Dorje, third Karmapa

Hail to Manjushri!   157
Rangjung Dorje, third Karmapa

A Vajra Song Aspiring to Tread the Footsteps
of the Heroes   158
Chone Lama Rinpoche

Little Tiger   160
Kelsang Gyatso, seventh Dalai Lama

An Adamantine Song on the Ever-Present   163
Longchen Rabjampa

On the Inner Practice of Secret Mantra   165
Drakpa Gyaltsen

At the Feet of the Lord of Dance   168
  Karma Trinley

In Response to a Request for Teaching on
Cause and Effect   171
  Drukpa Künlek

Experience of the Single Taste   173
  Za Paltrül Rinpoche

REFLECTIONS ON THE POET'S
OWN LIFE

Old Dog in the Wilderness   177
  Za Paltrül Rinpoche

A Song of Repentance and Disclosure   184
  Tsangpa Gyare

A Long Song of Sadness   186
  Chone Lama Rinpoche

Pay Heed, Pay Heed, O Zemey Tulku!   190
  Zemey Lobsang Palden

A Spring Day   192
  Kelsang Gyatso, seventh Dalai Lama

Glossary and Notes on the Poems   193
Biographies of the Poets   221
Bibliography   235
Sources for the Poems   237

FOREWORD

Tibetan Buddhism has a long tradition of what are called *nyamgur,* or "experiential songs," poems composed by realized masters articulating their deep spiritual experiences. Over the past four decades the world has come to know some of the great authors of this genre of Tibetan spiritual writing. Today, the *Hundred Thousand Songs of Milarepa*, the renowned verses of Tibet's much-loved religious poet; the experiential songs of the seventh Dalai Lama; and the autobiographical songs of Shapkar, among many others, can be read in English translations.

The poems presented in this anthology contain works by realized masters from all four schools of Tibetan Buddhism. They deal with such typically Buddhist contemplative themes as life's transience, the emptiness of intrinsic existence, and the meditator's yearning for solitude. This selection also conveys a sense of the wonderful combination of the personal and universal dimensions in the poet's experience. For example, Gungthang's provocative verses graphically describe the universal characteristics of aging and death, and Za Patrül's refreshingly frank lines express feelings with which many today can still identify.

Published here in English for the first time, the songs presented in this volume are some of the finest and most stirring verses ever written in Tibetan. For a Tibetan, these songs are not merely eloquent verses, but, more importantly, they have the power to evoke profound spiritual inspiration in the heart of the devout practitioner. Many of them were composed as spontaneous songs following a profound spiritual experience, so they carry a palpable sense of freshness and immediacy.

I am delighted to recommend *Songs of Spiritual Experience* to spiritual practitioners and ordinary readers alike, and pray that even in tranlation these verses will continue to be a source of comfort and inspiration as they have long been, in Tibetan.

TENZIN GYATSO
THE FOURTEENTH DALAI LAMA

PREFACE

This project was inspired by the example of those Tibetan spiritual master-poets who exemplified the fusion of a deep monastic rigor, a sharp philosophical acumen, and the love of poetic play, which are the marks of a true spiritual poet. It is to their memory that we dedicate this book. Our goal has been to create the first anthology in a Western language that offers samples from the rich heritage of Tibetan religious poetry from all the traditions and schools of Tibetan Buddhism.

This book is aimed at the general reader, who may approach these poems with no prior knowledge of Buddhism or of Tibet. The introduction is written to give as full an appreciation as possible of the place of poetry in the Tibetan spiritual tradition and in the lives of its practitioners. We have endeavored to let the poetry stand on its own in English. To this end, our overriding principle as translators has been to express the logic and thought process running through each poem, even (as rarely as possible) at the expense of our aesthetic sensibilities. However, we have chosen not to burden the reader with an overly scholarly apparatus. For example, all Tibetan words have been phoneticized instead of following the general scholarly convention that adopts Wylie's utterly unreadable transliteration. Likewise, we have respected poetry's prerogative to be free of footnotes and extensive commentaries or explanations. We have, nonetheless, provided a detailed glossary to help readers make sense of any obscure, technical, or specific references. In this sense the glossary also serves as a commentary. For the benefit of readers familiar with Tibetan, we include a bibliography and a list of sources that provides the page references for all the poems.

We would like to thank all those who have helped us in our work on these translations. Lobsang Shastri, of the Library of Tibetan Works and Archives in Dharamsala; Venerable Thupten Nyima (Zeng-kar Rinpoche); and Geshe Lobsang Chödar were instrumental in locating some of the less easily available texts in the original Tibetan. Those who read and commented upon our various drafts in English include Stephen Bachelor, Graham Coleman, Dante and Renée Els-ner, Chris Gilchrist, Grevel Lindop, John Peacock, and Andy Wist-reich. We have always taken their suggestions into account even if we have not always incorporated them. The cloisters of Girton College, Cambridge, provided a warm and supportive atmosphere for much of the work. Sophie Boyer-Langri and Silvia Elsner bore more than their fair share of consorts' duties. Not only did they allow us to lock ourselves away with pen and paper, but they even had to com-ment on the results! We would also like to express our deep appreci-ation to Eden Steinberg, our editor at Shambhala, for her invaluable help in ensuring that every part of the English text is made as clear and readable as possible.

Thupten Jinpa
Jaś Elsner

TRANSLATORS' INTRODUCTION

My own monastic training as a Geshe first began with a love for poetry.* From my childhood I have marveled at the beauty and perfection of the poetic forms and rhythms of the verses that were occasionally included in the school textbooks used by the exiled Tibetans in India. At that time, as a schoolboy of nine or ten years old, I could hardly follow the meaning, but I loved the sounds and memorized many of the verses. One name that was printed in all the textbooks was that of the chief editor, Zemey Rinpoche of Ganden. For some reason, I associated his name with these poems that I loved so much.

My life took me away from the regular pattern of the average Tibetan child growing up in exile in India in the late 1960s, after the Chinese invasion of Tibet and the flight of the Dalai Lama in 1959. I left school at the age of eleven to enter a monastery. It was not until I was seventeen that I rediscovered the name of Zemey Rinpoche. He was in fact one of the greatest living poets writing in the Tibetan language, as well as being a famous scholar and tantric master. I found that he was living in retirement just an hour's drive (by the Indian roads—about forty kilometers) from where my monastery was located near Mysore in south India. After a great deal of nervousness and soul-searching, I found the courage to approach an intermediary to arrange a meeting with Rinpoche. I desperately wanted to request that he teach me poetry. To this day, I remember our first meeting. I was very afraid that he would refuse to teach me, because he was so famous and because he was in semiretreat. It

*In this introduction, "we" stands for both translators and "I" for Thupten Jinpa.

I

is the custom to make an offering, but I had nothing special to offer. I took half a kilo of butter neatly packaged, prostrated before him, and offered him a white scarf. My first words were: "Please teach me poetry. You won't have to spend much time. I'm very bright!" Rinpoche was much amused at this immodest example of nervous forwardness and replied: "That's for me to judge!" Thus began my long association and spiritual relationship with the man who was to be the greatest influence on my life.

The point of this story is that it was through the root of poetry that my formal education into the rich world of Tibetan Buddhist learning and practice was begun. I was later, on the basis of my link with Rinpoche, to move to his great monastic university, Ganden, in south India and to enter the Geshe training in debate and metaphysics.

Perhaps out of all aspects of Tibetan culture, the poetry remains the least known in the outside world. There exist scholarly translations of some mystic poems, but apart from Milarepa and perhaps the notorious sixth Dalai Lama, people in the West have hardly heard of any of the great wealth of poets produced by Tibet since the eleventh century. Poetry has much to do with aesthetics, and perhaps the aesthetics behind the peculiarly Tibetan style of verse remain rather alien and need a careful and sympathetic introduction. The vastness of the landscape of Tibet, the harshness of the geography and climate, the sparsity of the population, and above all the brightness of nature's colors at an altitude of about four thousand meters, have all left their marks on the psyche of the Tibetan people. The poems intimate a certain haunting beauty combined with a profusion of imagery, striking, vivid, and at the same time simple. These qualities are at their most powerful when poets turn their inspiration to the great Buddhist themes of death, impermanence, and emptiness.

One characteristic of many Tibetan poems, which sets them apart from what one might ordinarily associate with poetry, is a certain quality of discursiveness. Many of the greatest Tibetan poems demand of the reader an attentiveness to a complex line of thought and philosophical reasoning, albeit in the heightened forms of verse combined with the inspiration of imagery. For the poet, the ideal reader is one whose reading of the poem becomes itself an act of meditation, penetrating the depths of human experience with an insight tempered by sensitivity. Clearly, sacred poetry of this sort, as opposed to the wonderful but much more popular verse of, say, the sixth Dalai Lama, is often written by monks inspired by the particular and sophisticated intellectual and meditative training of the monasteries, and is aimed specifically at the religious practitioner.

Many poems were addressed by meditators to themselves, as an act of inspiration through the hardships of a life dedicated to a single-pointed pursuit of enlightenment. When read by others, such poems appear as if they were the voice of the reader's inner being, exhorting him or her to attain that deeper state. These poems are often chanted by groups of monks or lay practitioners on meditation retreats. Though ostensibly articulating the poet's own personal experiences, they are read as resonances of higher states of being, open to all. For readers who may have had such religious experiences, reciting these verses may help attune their sensibilities to a greater clarity and lucidity. They may even recollect and reinforce the experience itself.

Many of the Tibetan *pujas*, or group prayers, are in fact collections of sacred verses. Sometimes, when one of the greater poems is recited in this way, it is not unusual to see people moved to tears. When Zemey Rinpoche used to give large public teachings of the Buddhist path, I remember that he would have the entire congregation sing some of the classic verses evoking impermanence and exhorting the individual to make human life meaningful. It is one of the most moving experiences to be in a large gathering of this sort and to see senior lamas and distinguished scholars weeping openly. Another use of these poems in dharma teachings is the selection of a specific stanza to bring home sharply a particular point. Take this example from the seventh Dalai Lama:

> A golden hill ablaze with yellow grass—
> silver mists hover round it like a belt;
> now it's here, now it's not.
> This brings to mind impermanence.

Or this from Gungthang:

> When aged parents mourn their young son's death,
> their bodies shaking and bent as bows,
> their hair white as a conch shell,
> who can maintain that the old die first?

The poetic vision crystallizes or condenses in a succinct and touching form what is taught in a didactic way. The choice of stanza to be quoted, as can be seen from the two examples here, makes a radical difference to the mood or emotive quality of what may be very similar themes, in this case the transient nature of life. This tradition of citing poetic evocations of the spiritual path even in didactic public teachings is very much alive today. For example, the present Dalai Lama's teachings to Tibetans (as distinct from his teachings to Westerners) abound with rich quotations of this sort.

In the traditional division of learning in Tibet, poetry is listed as one of the "five minor sciences" alongside prosody (the rules of meter), the knowledge of synonyms and antonyms, linguistics, and drama. Technically speaking, *nyengak*—the word we translate as "poetry" or "poetics"—literally means "eloquent speech" or "words of melody." *Nyengak* need not be composed only in verse: indeed, it exists in all three styles of composition as defined by the Tibetan literary theorists—that is, in metered verse, in prose, and in the intermixture of prose and verse. Broadly speaking, *nyengak* is a type of speech seen as especially eloquent and elaborate both in its literary form and in the ordering of the content to be described. It is thus a way of saying things—and in principle any subject or theme could be expressed in terms of *nyengak*. As a natural expression of human experience, the heightened language of poetry need not necessarily coincide with or be dependent on a systematized theory of poetics. In Tibetan culture, poetry certainly flourished before the formalized study and classification of it in terms of *nyengak*.

Perhaps a useful way of exploring the nature of poetry as a manner of heightened expression rather than a particular type of content or theme is to reflect on what is known in Tibetan poetics as the nine moods of poetic expression. These are inherited by the Tibetans from the Sanskrit tradition of nine *rasas* (meaning "moods" or "sentiments") that lie at the heart of classical Indian aesthetic theory, music, and poetics. The *rasa* of a verse, literally its "juice," is the essential pervading flavor of a given emotional situation. The great scholar Sakya Pandita Kunga Gyaltsen (1182–1251) defines the nine moods in his highly influential *Gateway of the Learned*. They are *gekpai nyam*, which is roughly equivalent to "elegant"; *pawai nyam*, or "majestic"; *midukpai nyam*, "repulsive"; *shegey kyi nyam*, "ironic" or "humorous"; *drakshül gyi nyam*, "wrathful" or "fierce"; *jikrung gi nyam*, "terrifying" or "awe-inspiring"; *nyingjai nyam*, "compassionate" or "empathetic"; *shiwai nyam*, "peaceful" or "pacifying"; and finally *mejung gi nyam*, which means "admiring." Any poem might combine some or all of these moods, or—depending on subject matter—one mood might dominate in any one poem. Of course, the list of nine is by no means exhaustive.

Grasping these moods is seen as an essential element in the appreciation of poetry, though the self-conscious application of a mood was not necessarily the way a poet would go about composing verses. For example, in this verse from a poem by Gungthang, there is a strong predominance of the ironic mood:

> The slowness of my dithering steps—
> not an important person's walk—
> is aging's unbalanced lurch
> burdened by decrepitude.

Indeed the whole poem, entitled "Ramblings of an Aged Man" is a wonderful example of a combination of the ironic and repulsive moods. Through these moods, the poem caricatures the condition of old age, making it seem repulsive. The purpose, however, is not to belittle age as such but to bring into sharper focus the urgency for spiritual change before it is too late.

Some poets are particularly renowned for the evocation of a mood—for instance, Gungthang was famous as an ironist; my own teacher, Zemey Rinpoche, was an accomplished writer in the majestic style; while the seventh Dalai Lama was a great master of the empathetic mood. The nine moods are a way of defining all Tibetan poetry, but the songs of spiritual experience with which we are concerned in this translation tend to avoid, for instance, the majestic and wrathful moods, which require a higher degree of stylistic embellishment. In spiritual verse, the predominance of the empathetic mood—with its effect of touching the heart directly—is not surprising.

On the literary and linguistic plane, one challenge of reading Tibetan poetry is to distinguish between the levels of discourse in a poem. Often the break between a metaphor and the topic to which it refers is not obvious. While some poems use pointers to distinguish between metaphor and referent (for instance, "as," "like," or "such as"), in many cases these are dropped, leaving the reader to tread carefully in order to follow the sense. A simple example of the use of simile is this, from Za Paltrül's wonderful poetic self-portrait:

When I first began meditating,
I felt a surge of bliss,
like a couple in love gazing on each other.

A much more complex example of the difficulties of wending one's way through similes is Changkya Rölpai Dorje's song on emptiness. Take this section, comprising one stanza and the beginning of the next:

This lunatic child
who lost his mother long ago
will soon learn by pure chance
that he just failed to recognize her.
She was with him all along!

Perhaps mother is the yes and no of emptiness

It is not until the beginning of the next verse that the reader has even the faintest intimation that the "mother" of the poem may be a metaphor for the ultimate nature of reality, which is emptiness in Mahayana Buddhism. The poem continues by reveling in the deliberate conflation of metaphor and referent when it evokes the image of the "father." Fortunately for the reader, most Tibetan poems articulate a complete thought (whether metaphor or referent or both) in a single stanza, usually consisting of four lines. Only in rare cases does a discrete thought extend over more than one verse. This gives the reader a great deal of help in grasping the sense, even in the most difficult poems.

Some things are possible in Tibetan verse that would be inconceivable in English. For example, in Tibetan it is possible for a consummate poet to write an entire stanza using only one vowel sound. Tsongkhapa's famous long poem entitled "A Literary Gem of Poetry" uses a single vowel in every stanza throughout the entire length. This is the poem from which come the famous lines:

> Good and evil are but states of the heart:
> When the heart is pure, all things are pure;
> When the heart is tainted, all things are tainted.
> So all things depend on your heart.

In the original Tibetan, this stanza uses only the vowel *a*. Of course, this kind of literary device can never be reproduced in a translation, whatever the virtuosity and command of the translator.

The original Tibetan word for the act of composition (be it verse, prose, or a mixture), *tsom*, came eventually to mean the writing of poetry. In early Tibetan there were several words for songs—*gur, lu,* and *she*—and of these it was ultimately *gur* that was used for the songs of spiritual experience with which we are concerned here. While the writing of verse goes back almost to the very origins of the Tibetan written script in the seventh century CE, possibly the first great poet whose works are universally acknowledged as poetic writings was Milarepa (1040–1123). His poems, although among the earliest, are still among the highest examples of *gur*. By any standards, Milarepa was a master poet; indeed, the very sophistication and excellence of his work implies that he leaned on a richly developed oral tradition. *The Hundred Thousand Songs of Milarepa,* which is an autobiographical account of his interaction with the world and his path to enlightenment, opened the way for a profusion of poetic writing, especially by a number of gifted students and imitators. These songs by Milarepa were collected only in the fifteenth century, by Tsangnyön Heruka (1452–1507), but they must have been widely disseminated in fragments (and various versions) before that time. Although the Indian mystic writings of the *doha* tradition, especially the *Royal Songs of Saraha*, must have lent some influence to the indigenous Tibetan practice exemplified by Milarepa, nonetheless the great flowering of Tibetan poetry in the twelfth and thirteenth centuries—works by masters such as Drakpa Gyaltsen,

Natsok Rangdröl, and Tsangpa Gyare—can be seen as a truly Tibetan phenomenon. However, one act was to transform Tibetan poetry forever: this was the introduction of the great Sanskrit manual of poetics called *Kavyadarsha*, or the "Mirror of Poetry," written by Dandin in the seventh century CE and translated into Tibetan in the thirteenth century.

The *Kavyadarsha* is a remarkable work of synthesis that brought together the vast array of poetic traditions in the Sanskrit language from the north and south of the Indian subcontinent. Its principal concerns were the detailed codification of all the different uses of metaphor in poetry and how they affect poetic meaning, and a lengthy discussion of the linguistic skills—almost the word games—involved in the mastery of rhymes, puns, and acrostics (including the deliberate manipulation of all kinds of literary effects across a poem's lines and meters). So important was this masterpiece of formalization that it was translated more than once into Tibetan and attracted numerous commentaries by Tibetan scholars and poets. In his *Gateway for the Learned*, Sakya Pandita had already introduced many important elements of Indian poetics based on his extensive knowledge of the Sanskrit sources. The other key figures in this great act of transmission were the translators Shongtön Lotsawa Dorje Gyaltsen (thirteenth century) and Pangtön Lotsawa Lodrö Tenpa (1276–1342), both of whom also wrote commentaries. Among the Tibetan commentaries, those by the fifth Dalai Lama (1617–1682), Mipham Gelek Namgyal (b.1618), and Khamtrül Tenpai Nyima (b. 1745) are considered today to be the most authoritative. In my studies under Zemey Rinpoche, I relied on Mipham's commentary as the main textbook in my study of the *Kavyadarsha*.

Each verse of the *Kavyadarsha* consists of an exposition of a particular use of metaphor or a poetic device. The method of study is for the teacher to explain the intricacies of the verses to be covered that day and to present sample poems by great masters illustrating how they conform to the rules of poetics set down in the *Kavyadarsha*. Students are then expected to read the commentary and to write their own sample stanzas for each of the forms studied that day. These are presented to the teacher, who will make comments and corrections. This process may take a couple of hours daily over more than six months if one book of the *Kavyadarsha* is to be covered in a single stretch. This is how I studied under Zemey Rinpoche, first near Mysore when he was in retreat and later in Ganden when I followed him there. As far as I know, this method of study is that employed by all Tibetan poets since the thirteenth century, when the *Kavyadarsha* was first translated. It is a sad thought that my generation will probably be the last to have studied poetry in this traditional way. In the modern world, even in the Tibetan monasteries of India, there is so little time. And in the conventional Tibetan schools, so many other more modern subjects (including learning English) have to take priority.

In the actual process of learning how to write verses, there is an emphasis on a very strict adherence to the forms specified and defined in the *Kavyadarsha*. The teacher carefully points out to the student if there is any conflation of more than one use of metaphor, as defined by the manual, in any one stanza. This is because such conflation betrays a confusion in the mind of the student with regard to the specific nature of a particular use of metaphor. In addition, the teacher's corrections will also suggest alternative words and perhaps a change in the order of a particular expression in the stanzas. I have always marveled at the way even a very simple alteration made by Rinpoche would bring to life a stanza that I myself had written. The image that comes to mind is that I had drawn a face, but Rinpoche's ever-so-small addition added the smile that lightened up the whole expression. For a student, going verse by verse through the *Kavyadarsha* is a laborious process. I still remember the hours of agonizing effort in getting together even one decent-sounding verse.

Yet when Rinpoche or his teacher, Kyabje Trijhang Rinpoche, wrote poetry, the stanzas were so fluid, spontaneous, and free. Although the process of learning is so labored and rigorous, later—when you compose a poem—you no longer think about the injunctions of the *Kavyadarsha*; somehow the training has become innate.

Obviously the introduction of such a formalized and rigorous analysis of poetic forms was to transform the face of poetry in Tibet. The spontaneous and fluid songs of Milarepa and his followers, full of vernacular terms and not so far from the language of the ordinary Tibetan, gave way to a much more stylized, refined, and elaborate poetic diction. In effect, the predominantly oral poetry of the eleventh, twelfth, and thirteenth centuries was transformed into a fully fledged literary and scholarly tradition. Undoubtedly the resources of Tibetan poetry were hugely enriched by the deep technical expertise generated by this systematization. At the same time, on the level of content, the use of the *Kavyadarsha*, with its encyclopedic grasp of Sanskrit poetry, gave access to the rich world of Indian mythology and symbolism. The fact that poetics was now a formalized discipline was immensely significant for the clarity, refinement, and linguistic elegance of poetic forms. The formalization of poetry as a literary discipline led to a far greater emphasis on strict adherence to rhythm and meter in the writing of verse.

One of the effects of the "Sanskritization" of Tibetan verse was to turn its reception into an activity of the elite. Especially in its abundant use of multiple synonyms and its allusions to myths from Indian literature, poetry demanded much greater sophistication and learning on the part of the reader. References to *garuda* or Mount Meru, for example, carry a resonance beyond Buddhism to the mythical range of Indian culture. Synonyms are particularly difficult, since it required a certain amount of learning to know that "the one that increases the tides," for instance, means "the moon." In fact, the lavish use of synonyms can be a disaster for the translator, since to keep them in their most allusive form renders a poem virtually incomprehensible in many cases. Fortunately, the songs of spiritual experience generally tend to be sparse in their employment of extravagant language.

Traditionally, this transformation of Tibetan poetry has been regarded very positively. In poetry in general it is hard to see any serious defects in the impact of Sanskrit poetics. But for the poems with which this book is concerned—songs of spiritual experience and meditative realization, the kinds of songs for which Milarepa had already set a virtually supreme model by any standards—there was a price. The essence of spiritual songs is their spontaneity, their immediacy, the momentary capturing of a transformed state of mind, while all the rules of meter, metaphor, and language encouraged by formalization can (and did) have the effect of hindering the natural flow of spontaneity in favor of technically refined forms. To a degree, mastery of form was emphasized at the cost of immediacy of content.

In the beginning of my study of the *Kavyadarsha*, one problem that troubled me was the thought that this was all so difficult. Before my formal studies, I had written verses quite easily and spontaneously— poems that I thought at the time were rather beautiful. Now it took forever to write even a single verse, which felt labored rather than free. I raised this issue with Zemey Rinpoche, implying that all this mechanical learning was more of a hindrance than a help, that it was obstructing my natural flow. Rinpoche replied that true perfection comes from the harnessing of a natural gift to a skillful command. The rigors of the *Kavyadarsha*, he said, offer an incomparably deeper resourcefulness to the poet; pure spontaneity without discipline remains at the level of a child. The child may offer a direct insight, but it is haphazard, the result of chance; if the skilled poet can combine expertise with the freshness of a child, he becomes a master. After my study of the *Kavyadarsha*, when I looked back on my old verses, I came to appreciate his point.

This problem of the potential loss of spontaneity has never been explicitly recognized in writings about formalized poetry, perhaps because after the assimilation of the *Kavyadarsha*'s poetics everything definable as poetry was of the formalized kind. Yet there seems to have been an implicit acknowledgment of the conflict between form and spontaneity. Even after the arrival of Sanskrit poetics, the tradition of writing experiential songs continued. Perhaps the most important means through which Milarepa's spontaneous tradition was preserved was the assigning of a specific set of rhythms almost exclusively for the use of experiential songs, or what became known as the medium of *nyamgur*. In conventional Tibetan verse, there are two principal meters, one of nine and one of seven syllables. They may be expressed like this, with the accent falling always on the first syllable of each foot:

--/--/--/---

and

--/--/---

Common to this conventional style of writing is that the last foot always has three syllables. The *nyamgur* rhythms deliberately defy this convention—and in particular its insistence on regularity of rhythm and cadence. In contrast, they may be expressed like this, again with the emphasis on the first syllable of each foot:

--/-/--
--/--/--
-/--/--/---
--/--/---/--
--/--/--/---/--

The last three of these meters are the most famous, employed by spiritual poets from Milarepa himself to modern masters such as Trijhang Rinpoche and Zemey Rinpoche.

Here, in case they may aid the reader in finding a feeling for the rhythms of Tibetan spiritual verse, are transliterations of two stanzas in the original Tibetan from poems in our collection in some of the meters most favored by the mystic poets. First, a stanza from Gungthang's poem on impermanence (p. 33) using the meter -/--/--/--- in each line:

> Lo / da wa / 'di la / 'di nang gi
> lay / jha jhe / tshung su / tshü jhe nay
> lar / tsang ma'I / chö shig / jhe nyam pa
> di / tham ce / lu wai / phung dre yin

Second, a stanza from Za Paltrül's poem on life's transience (p. 31), which uses the meter -- /-- /-- /---/-- in each line:

> Kye ma / trul nang / khor we / yun ring du / lü lü
> trul tok / tsa wa / ma chö / nyam thak gi / dro la
> tshung med / drin chan / la ma'i / thug je yi / sik nay
> a thay / trul pa / shik par / jhin gyi rang / log shig

While the conventional rhythms of Tibetan verse are particularly suited for chanting and recitation, the peculiar characteristic of the meters employed for the experiential songs is that they are closer to the melodies of music. They are less regular and monotonous, as well as varying their cadences and emphases. This is perhaps because their rhythms resonate with echoes of traditional Tibetan folk songs and music. The songlike quality of these meters helped to preserve the sense of naturalness and immediacy so central to poems of spiritual experience. These songs are by no means the only Tibetan religious verse, but they form a special and very important category. The types of religious verse in general include *töpa*, hymns or works of praise to one's guru or higher beings; *tokjö*, stylized biographies of highly evolved spiritual masters written almost invariably in a mix of verse and prose; *lapja*, versified but didactic instructions; *tagur*, philosophical verses (see the examples in the section entitled "Echoes of Emptiness"); *mönlam*, aspirational prayers (such as Tsongkhapa's "A Prayer for the Flourishing of Virtues," p. 129); and, of course, *nyamgur*, the experiential songs—the main focus of the present anthology.

More than being merely a subgenre of poetry, the songs of spiritual experience are a profound element of meditative practice and inspiration. Just as the continuing lineage of writing spontaneous poetry acted as a counterforce to the impact of the rigid formalization of verse writing, so in the lives of individuals the spontaneity of the experiential songs was a most important counterbalance to rigorous philosophical training and analysis. For instance, Zemey Rinpoche's life embodies an interesting marriage of the detailed precision and clarity of the rational analytic training of the monastic university tradition with a deep yearning for the freedom and openness of experience available to the solitary hermit and evoked by the experiential songs. In his later life (when I met him and studied with him), Rinpoche had retired from a string of official posts and duties to a life of meditative semiretreat devoted to solitude and verse writing. One of the practices of both Zemey Rinpoche and his own teacher, Kyabje Trijhang Rinpoche, in retirement toward the end of their lives, was not only to compose songs but to sing them to small groups of close disciples. To hear a beautiful song sung by the poet himself is a truly wonderful experience.

One particular aspect of experiential poetry is its power in creating strong affinities between a guru and his disciple. One reason for the closeness of Zemey Rinpoche with his own guru, Trijhang Rinpoche, was the fact that they both shared a deep passion for poetry. When I arrived in Ganden to live in Zemey Rinpoche's household, I had the privilege of being given access to a special relationship with Trijhang Rinpoche, despite the fact that he was a tutor to His Holiness the Dalai Lama and one of the most senior masters of the entire

Gelukpa tradition, while I was just a newcomer. After hearing about my interest in poetry from Zemey Rinpoche, one day Trijhang Rinpoche called me to come to see him with all the exercise stanzas I had written during my poetry lessons with Zemey Rinpoche. He was an old man at that time, tall and thin, with sharp features for a Tibetan but a gaze of caring gentleness. And he had an amazing voice, soft, deep, and melodious. I said, "I feel very embarrassed to show these efforts to such a towering figure in the world of Tibetan poetry." He said, "Don't worry. I will read your poetry, not from a position of mastery, but as if I were following a learner's path of progression." To my surprise, he called for refreshments and we had tea together. He teased me by saying to his attendant, Palden-la, who had a good appreciation of literature, "Come and meet our new young poet!"

In our next meeting, again over tea, he said "I have read all your poems," which surprised me, since it was a great compliment. "You must know," he continued, "that we poets are a small band of people. To outsiders we may seem silly or childish. It is very rare to have the sensibility to appreciate poetry; but it is rarer still to have the gift to be able to write poems. You must treasure this gift and nurture it. One way in which you can be in constant touch with your poetic dimension is to compose a verse every day. It can be on any theme, or relate to any experience in the day." Of course, I never managed to compose verse as regularly or freely as he suggested, but his comments give an insight into the great poet's cultivation of his treasured vocation.

Since then, I have always felt a special affinity with Trijhang Rinpoche. I have read all his poems, which were published as part of his collected works. This story indicates the special bonds that a poet in the Tibetan tradition may feel for someone with a poetic sensibility. Despite the huge gap in age, hierarchy, and spiritual attainment, Trijhang Rinpoche—one of the very highest lamas in the

Geluk order—made time to take tea with an aspiring poet. This is rather as if a first-year novice in a Roman Catholic monastery were invited to tea in the Vatican.

The key themes of Tibetan experiential songs touch on the most personal aspects of the spiritual path and on the profound insights into the nature of reality that are the fruits of the path. On the personal side, the yearning for solitude and recollections of the absent guru are prominent, as well as some striking—and even highly ironic—reflections on the poet's life. On the philosophical side, perhaps the key topics are evocations of the transient and contingent nature of human existence, as well as the great Mahayana theme of emptiness. There is also a strong mystic tradition (going back to Milarepa himself) in these songs, which evokes and celebrates the multiple dimensions of the evolving states of consciousness associated with tantra. The free play of the songs of spontaneous experience in confronting these themes allows them to transcend the differences between the four major lineages of Tibetan Buddhism— Nyingma, Kagyü, Sakya, and Geluk.

Given that all the poets in this anthology saw themselves first and foremost as seekers on the Buddhist path to enlightenment, a few words of introduction to Buddhism may be appropriate. Like many ancient Indian religious traditions, Buddhism sees sentient beings— including human beings—as revolving in a perpetual cycle of birth and death known as samsara. This form of existence is characterized and burdened by an underlying and inescapable sense of suffering, or at best dissatisfaction. At the root of what is called the ocean of samsara lies a fundamental delusion, often described simply as ignorance. The path of enlightenment taught by the Buddha aims to cut the chains tying beings to this fundamental ignorance and hence to free them from the ocean of cyclic existence. The key element of the Buddhist path is developing a profound insight into the nature of this kind of existence and hence opening the way to spiritual freedom. The very first sermon taught by the Buddha sought to explore the process whereby one might move from suffering to happiness, from ignorance to knowledge. He taught that there is suffering and that suffering has its origin, that there is a cessation to suffering and that there exists a path to that cessation: this is called the four noble truths.

At the heart of the Buddha's teaching on the nature of suffering lies the insight that existence is characterized by impermanence and dissatisfaction, and that there is no permanent self experiencing the world. Clinging to a sense of permanence or selfhood is precisely what the Buddha meant by fundamental ignorance. Historically, the numerous schools of Buddhism that developed after the Buddha's death can be seen as representing slightly different interpretations and unravelings of this core teaching of the Buddha. Tibet inherited the so-called Mahayana development of Buddhism from India, whose key features were an emphasis on universal compassion as the primary motivation for spiritual practice and a philosophical elaboration of the concept of no-self as understood in terms of the theory of emptiness. In fact, these two aspects of the path are known in the Tibetan tradition as skillful means or method (compassion) and wisdom (the insight into emptiness). The path to enlightenment is unattainable without a genuine unification of compassion and wisdom.

The particular form of Mahayana adopted by all four schools of Tibetan Buddhism, and hence by the poets in this anthology, encompasses Vajrayana, the so-called adamantine vehicle, which can be broadly described as esoteric or tantric Buddhism. It is in the practice of this dimension of the spiritual path that we find visions and experiences that may best be called mystic. Common to all the experiential songs is a special mystic's perspective on the world. As Gungthang says in his long poem called the "Tree Similes":

He who sees all things as metaphor,
that yogin is never starved of scripture.

If the practitioner cultivates the right way of seeing the world, every experience is a guru—a teacher in the path to enlightenment. This perspective, which is very evident in the imagery of the poems on impermanence and emptiness, is the special characteristic of the experiential songs in the path to enlightenment. The poems give life and color to the insights of the teaching gained through rational discourse, they open the mind of the practitioner to the metaphoric dimension where all things are signs, and they bring home the central themes of the great Buddhist teachings through their strong personal engagement.

Because they are simultaneously so personal and so metaphoric, the songs of spiritual experience form a unique category of religious literature in Tibet. Unlike philosophical treatises and verses, they need not be subjected to rigorous evaluation of their intellectual content. In approaching these songs, readers would not instinctively use criteria such as consistency and precision that they would normally apply. It is as if the metaphorical perspective and the almost idiosyncratically personal nature of the poet's experience combined with a certain poetic license provide unlimited liberty. For this reason, some of the tenets of Buddhist doctrine appear to be freely flouted. For example, there is a repeated yearning for what poets call the essence, the ever-presence, primordial purity, the self-arisen awareness, the unchanging nature, even the absolute. Philosophically speaking, such concepts are untenable in mainstream Buddhist thinking, which constantly warns against the dangers of metaphysical reification. Some of the experiential songs even appear to possess overtones of theism, which is certainly anathema to Buddhist thinking. Yet in the context of the spontaneous poetic expression of deep spiritual experience, all such metaphors are permissible. They are evocative, and—through their inspiration—they may open the reader to an awakening to what is in principle indescribable. The language here is no longer referential but predominantly metaphoric.

This freedom perhaps reaches its height in the poems that re-count the experiential states of tantra. Often in between long medi-tative sessions of tantric visualization, meditator-poets have written intimations of their visions of a transformed mode of being where everything is perceived as divine. The freedom of the genre of expe-riential songs allows a creative play of imagination and fantasy—the very qualities that tantric meditation itself seeks to exploit. In tantra the poems have a special role, since they are inspired directly by the altered states of consciousness experienced by practitioners, and they are themselves used to help meditators in tantric visualization by giving an added texture or tone both through the music of the song and through the color of a direct and personal vision evoked in the poem.

It is ironic, perhaps, since many of the poets were celibate monks, that the songs are often pregnant with sexual imagery. Take this example from a poem by Chone Lama Rinpoche, a famous ascetic and practitioner of the early twentieth century, known for his dedi-cation to life as a monk:

> May my mind be always intoxicated
> by drinking insatiably the nectar—
> the delicious taste of sexual play
> between the hero in his utter ecstasy
> and his lover, the lady emptiness.
>
> By entering deep into the sphere of voidness,
> may I be endowed with the power of cleansing
> this foul odor, grasping body, speech, and mind as ordinary,
> through the yoga perceiving all as divine.

In these verses the vivid sexual imagery is inextricable from a series of fundamental aspects of tantra—the aesthetic sense of emptiness; the union of emptiness and bliss; the transmutation of the "three doors" of the practitioner's body, speech, and mind; and the perception of all appearances as divine. In some cases, for example the work of Drukpa Künlek, crude sexual imagery may sometimes be used to shock the reader's sensibilities. The line between mystic consciousness and overt eroticism may occasionally seem blurred. However, the immense popularity of Drukpa Künlek and the recognition of his saintliness suggest a healthy lack of excessive piety in the religious sentiments of the Tibetan people.

In part the emphasis on sexual imagery occurs because in the Buddhist mystic tradition of tantra there is an understanding that the ultimate experience of enlightenment is orgasmic in a profound sense, that the sexual energies transformed are the means to attain enlightenment. According to this view, there is a close affinity between the states of consciousness during deep sleep, sexual climax, death, and enlightenment itself. They are all stages at which the mind glimpses the most natural and pure states of consciousness; they are all stages far removed from the ordinary or habitual conditionings and concepts. In part, moreover, the sexual imagery is a potent metaphor for the cultivation of a perspective fundamental to tantra—namely the nonduality (or union) of a mind in which the experience of bliss is united with the understanding of emptiness. What metaphor can be more powerful for the evoking of the notion of unifying all aspects of one's being than the image of male and female in sexual union?

This anthology is a small selection from the vast world of experiential songs, which are themselves but one genre of Tibetan poetry. Even as a collection of songs of spiritual experience, it is by no means exhaustive. I have been guided by the principle of giving the reader a taste of the wide range of poems reflecting a variety of themes, styles, and temperaments. The selection spans a long time period, from the eleventh century until our own time, and includes poets from all the four main spiritual lineages of Tibetan Buddhism. Any reader familiar with Tibetan spontaneous songs will immediately notice how small is the space devoted here to three great mystic poets—Milarepa, Drukpa Künlek, and Shapkar. This is deliberate. It is simply because good translations into English already exist of the entire corpus of these three masters. These three belong to a class of spiritual practitioners known as wandering mystics. In the present collection, special attention is given to two other wandering mystic poets—Za Paltrül Rinpoche and Chone Lama Rinpoche, both from the end of the nineteenth and the beginning of the twentieth centuries.

Inevitably the selection betrays my own poetic tastes. To a degree these were informed by the influence of Zemey Rinpoche. He introduced me to a number of poets of whom he was particularly fond who did not belong to the Geluk tradition within which both he and I were monks. He would often quote verses freely by Za Paltrül, Milarepa, Drukpa Künlek, and Shapkar, from the Nyingma and Kagyü schools. In fact, Za Paltrül ranked among his most admired writers. Perhaps his most frequent quotation—and certainly his favorite lines—was this couplet from a long poem by Za Paltrül:

> Haughty youth, with not the faintest thought of death,
>   beware!
> Between a man and a corpse is but the slender line of breath.

To a modern reader, a major omission will be obvious. There is only one woman poet in our collection—Machik Labdrön. Unfortunately, she is unique in being the only universally renowned woman mystic who composed experiential songs. I do not myself know of other female poets of her stature, and my researches in the archives of the Library of Tibet in Dharamsala have failed to turn up any others. Traditional historians of religion in Tibet are silent on the question of the role of women in the development of Buddhist thought and practice, as well as in literature. For whatever reason, it seems to be a sad truth of Tibetan literary history that few women have been writers. There have been a number of major women mystics and great practitioners; however, they seem not to have felt the urge to compose verse, or at least their poems have been lost or remain only in manuscript form and have not yet been published.

The guiding principle behind our selection has been the desire to present a comprehensive range of the themes of the songs of spiritual experience, which together present a full picture of the experiential world of the path to enlightenment. To reflect this spirit we group the poems we have chosen thematically (rather than chronologically or by author) into categories that we perceive as representing the key aspects of this spiritual path, its manifestation in meditation experience, and its fruition. The selection of the themes and their ordering broadly reflects the way the personal path of a spiritual seeker unfolds, as idealized in all the four major traditions of Tibetan Buddhism. The first section is the evocation of impermanence—which arouses the sense of urgency to renounce the material world and seize the opportunity to enter a spiritual life. The vividness and the sense of revulsion that are apparent in many of these poems are an attempt to shock the reader into waking from the slumber of complacency. A radical awareness of death and the transient nature of life calls for the need to change.

The second section consists of poems expressing the yearning for solitude. Once the practitioner is already awake through the awareness of death, there is the need for the time and space to dedicate oneself to a life of single-pointed meditation and insight. This ideal is embodied in the poet's yearning for solitude, both metaphorical and literal. The third section, "Calling the Guru from Afar," explores the meditator's need for inspiration and resources as he or she develops the path of the solitary mystic. These songs are often strongly emotional. The guru called upon may be the practitioner's teacher or sometimes the idealized vision of an enlightened teacher—even the Buddha within. We include in this section a poem by Zemey Rinpoche written at the death of his own guru, Trijhang Rinpoche, calling for his swift reincarnation.

The fourth section concerns the experiential insight into emptiness, which we call "Echoes of Emptiness." The meditator—motivated, in solitude, and inspired by the guru's blessing—turns his mind to the great task of the search for enlightenment, namely, penetrating the ultimate nature of reality. In Mahayana Buddhism this is understood as a deepening process of freeing the mind of the ingrained tendencies of grasping at the self and the world. The antidote to these profound habits of attachment is to cultivate the view of emptiness. By "emptiness" is meant the absolute negation of the independent being that we ascribe to our own existence and to the world in our normal worldview. As can be inferred from the poems in this section, it is by no means an easy process. It demands insight into reality, the absorption to follow the subtle movements of the mind, the concentration to trace the meandering path of reasoning, and above all, sensitivity to the openness of human experience. In fact, there is a case for calling these songs philosophical verses. Because of this, the poems in this section may be the most difficult in this anthology.

The fifth section, "Steps on the Path to Awakening," contains poems whose themes pertain to other key aspects of the Buddhist path, such as compassion, renunciation, the overcoming of worldly concerns, and applying antidotes to negative tendencies. These poems intimate the scope of the graduated path to enlightenment (lamrim) in Tibetan Buddhism, which can be seen as suggesting a series of progressively developed states of meditation. The sixth section, "Visions of Mystic Consciousness," consists of songs of tantric realization, which articulate the ultimate vision of full awakening according to Tibetan Buddhism. Certainly the tantric poems demand a more metaphorical perspective than some of the other experiential songs, and may seem in parts rather more obscure. This is due partly to the veiling of the teachings within the mystic tradition and partly also to the series of terms specific to the language of tantra. In recognition of this difficulty, we endeavor to explain some of the key issues in the glossary and notes on the poems.

The fifth and sixth sections of our anthology relate to the final development of the mystic's path once the understanding of emptiness has dawned. It is then necessary to root out the deepest worldly tendencies and to generate the radical compassion of the Buddha. Thus, insight alone is not sufficient; there must be what is called the union of method and wisdom, which is to say, of insight and compassion. The fifth section also includes a classic example of a prayer of aspiration. Not only are such prayers recited by many people, including lay practitioners as well as monks, but they are also memorized as sources of inspiration. To a contemporary reader, Tsongkhapa's famous "Prayer for the Flourishing of Virtues" (p. 129) gives an insight into the deepest ideals of a dedicated Tibetan Buddhist practitioner; it presents a map of progressive development on the path. Beyond this, the mystic must utterly transform the very root of his identity and the perceptions that arise from it. From the ordinary patterns of action and reaction that make up our psyche and emotional life, the meditator must move toward a divine state of altered consciousness where all realities, including one's own self, are manifested in their enlightened forms. In other words, the meditator must perfect all dimensions of his or her identity and experience, including rationality, emotion, intuition, and even sexuality. This, in Tibetan Buddhism, is the mystical realm of tantra.

The final section, entitled "Reflections on the Poet's Own Life," includes a group of wonderful poems that look back from the vantage point of a certain spiritual maturity, and even old age, onto the life of the poet. Through the most intensely personal of reflections, they give a panoramic—and occasionally surprising—view over the poet's own progress or failings on the spiritual path. Often these poems take on a self-deprecating mood, which is designed to give the poet a sense of final urgency and acceleration on the path as life draws near its end. They may be designed as much for the disciples as for the guru, since the presentation of the teacher's hardships leaves no room for illusion about the easiness of the spiritual endeavor. Therefore, the modern reader need not take these poems as literally autobiographical; rather, the "I" of these self-portraits is a carefully chosen persona.

It is a matter of great sadness that the generation of Trijhang Rinpoche and Zemey Rinpoche—itself a time of great flowering of Tibetan religious poetry within Tibet—is perhaps the end of an era. The early twentieth century saw a renaissance of spiritual poetry, partly inspired by such superb practitioners as Chone Lama and Za Paltrül. But the 1950 Communist Chinese invasion of Tibet, the subsequent upheavals, and the final flight of the Dalai Lama and other senior lamas (including both Zemey Rinpoche and Trijhang Rinpoche) in 1959 have drawn what seems like an irrevocable line beneath the personal tradition of passing on the spirit of poetry from master to student, of a poet's grooming of successors in the way Trijhang Rinpoche groomed Zemey Rinpoche. Although these poets still wrote some of their finest verse in their Indian exile, the difficult conditions and new realities of a displaced community have taken their toll. The practice of poetry is simply not as high a priority as the passing on of the dharma and the ensurance of survival. But its loss is a great tragedy for Tibet's cultural heritage—and inside Tibet, it is most unlikely that the tradition of religious poetry (as distinct from other kinds of verse) has survived the deliberate persecution of the Chinese authorities.

. . .

Inevitably, in presenting an anthology like this, the issue of the problems of translation arises. For example, we have felt compelled to leave a number of terms untranslated from their original Sanskrit or Tibetan, such as *dharma, rikpa, samsara, nirvana,* and so forth. We have tried to keep them to a minimum—but they are key terms in Buddhist thought for which no simple English translation exists. Quite apart from the inelegance of using a lengthy phrase every time to convey, say, the meaning of *karma,* doing so might break the succinctness of a train of thought pursued by the poet. We have, however, provided a glossary with notes for the reader's assistance.

The experiential poems posit a particular challenge to the translator, since they combine a deliberate use of vernacular and even colloquial terms or expressions with quite complex esoteric vocabulary. It is easy for translators to be tempted into reading too much high mysticism into what may sometimes be a very ordinary or simple expression of feeling. Ultimately, one effect of the experiential songs is their union of the spiritual with the everyday, so that sacred experience is expressed through the popular and even the familiar.

It is universally acknowledged that poetry is untranslatable (in the strict sense of the word) from one language to another. In translations, there is always a third person (in our case, two) between the reader and the author, raising the nagging question of who is actually the author of any poem one might be reading. In perusing any of the songs we have translated, we ourselves are painfully aware of how much has been lost on the level of melody, rhythm, and literary beauty; of how many puns, ironic wordplays, and stylistic devices have been jettisoned. Our dominant principal has been, despite the loss of so much of the linguistic aesthetics (for example, we have deliberately chosen not to emulate the original meters in English), to capture both the sense and the mood of the original. We have tried to be particularly sensitive to the temperament specific to the work of an individual poet. Of course, in cases where an image may allude to multiple meanings, we have been forced to be reductive in our choice of an English version, but we have rigorously striven to keep to the principal meaning of the Tibetan—working on drafts and revisions with the original Tibetan poem in front of us as both a guide and a ruler. If we have managed to capture any aspect of the haunting beauty of which we spoke earlier, or to intimate to the reader some sense of the refined dimensions of spiritual conscious-ness that form the world of the experiential songs, we would con-sider our modest efforts to have succeeded.

Evocations
of Life's Transience

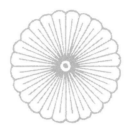

from *Tunes on the Absence of Elaborations*

Za Paltrül Rinpoche (1808–1887)

O unfortunate beings grasping at the appearances of delusion,
seeing this world of suffering as *real*, momentary, or eternal,
may we be touched by the kindness of the peerless guru,
blessed in the experience of all things as teaching.

From birth everyone charges in haste without obstruction
on the road that leads through a narrow gorge toward the lord
    of death:
wrathful and glaring with eyes striking terror,
he wields a dagger and hoists a black lasso.
Lo, we who come from the land of the living,
we never dream that we could be no more.
Sowing the earth with white grain hoarded in sacks,
we are confident of a crop at the time of harvest;
yet, knowing not the deadline of the farmer's life,
can we be sure he'll be here to drink the harvest wine?

Haughty youth, with not the faintest thought of death,
    beware!
Between a man and a corpse is but the slender line of breath.
The parting of body and spirit at a young man's decease
is easy, but they say it's full of sorrow and fear.

O beautiful maidens adorned with jewelry and flowers,
do you consider that soon you'll be gray-haired and aged?
No hiding place conceals you from the stealthy grasp of aging.
What can you do? The pain of aging can be worse than death!

This body that we nurture is but a source of illness;
adversity attacks it unannounced, the piercing arrows
of pain slice the bonds of body and spirit, as an offering to the
   lord of death.
The corpse we fear so much is in truth right before us.

O kind gurus, look with compassion on the unfortunate beings
who've failed to cut the roots of all deceptions,
who've been fooled for long lifetimes in the cycle of samsara.
May they be blessed to unbind the knots of delusion.

A Meditation on Impermanence

Gungthang Tenpai Drönme (1762–1822)

I salute the supreme gurus.
They create in the glorious sky of bliss
thick, enveloping clouds of emanations,
raining showers of profound and vast teachings.

Oh, this human existence I have found this once
is slipping away through my own fingers;
it's time now to tread the path to freedom.
Catch this hook revealing transience.

The thought that "in this year and that month
I will organize and tie up the loose ends
and then engage in real practice"
is the devil that causes all downfalls.

Mundane tasks are like ripples on water,
as one dissolves, another appears;
they multiply as they are pursued.
Doesn't wisdom lie in ending this?

Before "tomorrow's dharma practice,"
the dying moment of "today" may come.
Let us deceive ourselves no more.
If we wish to practice, the time is now!

Of all past Buddhas and bodhisattvas,
whose deeds pervade the three realms—

nothing remains except their names.
All are teachers of impermanence.

Kings and ministers inflated by power
whose garlanded deeds are the stuff of myth,
when unprobed seem real enough,
yet in all three realms not a trace remains.

When lifelong friends, our equals,
are suddenly taken by the enemy, death,
what certainty, what confidence
that we ourselves can sidestep death?

If so stupid an animal as a sheep
shakes when its kindred meet the butcher's knife;
how much more stupid is the man who fails
to grasp this truth in his own life.

Death is the unavoidable fact. The man
who fails to grasp this even when before his eyes
(there is no need of proof or scripture here),
he is called the wide-eyed blind!

The assembly of family and friends,
like fallen leaves collected by the wind,
soon will scatter in the mountains and plains
never again to meet. This is their last gathering.

The congregation of people at the marketplace
is like the bees at the end of fall; they disperse
as soon as they get together. This too,
for the wise, is a teaching on impermanence.

Nature is a conjurer, changing day to day
the colors of mountains and valleys
through seasons of "summer" and "winter."
This too is a teaching of impermanence!

The turquoise dancing water
with a perpetual murmur of waves,
when imprisoned beneath the cage of winter ice,
is like a girl crying for help with muffled voice.

Joyful fields of flowers humming with bees
when attacked by morning frost in autumn
become a deserted ghostly plain.
They wail in agony before the hail's onslaught.

The white and the black rats, day and night
in turns consume life's fragile straw.
We too step every instant
ever closer to the enemy, death.

When aged parents mourn their young son's death,
their bodies shaking and bent as bows,
their hair white as a conch shell,
who can maintain that the old die first?

Rich man struck by adversity,
like a ripe crop blighted by hail,
your pleas may not be answered
even by servants whom you have long fed.

When the best friend of today
becomes tomorrow's worst enemy

on account of a few unguarded words,
here end feelings of closeness and distance.

The attraction of wealth and prosperity
is like a glowing lamp to a moth;
with its seductive face of beauty and desire
it cuts the jugular of lasting happiness.

In brief, death's coming is soon and definite,
yet its timing cannot be foretold,
nothing can reverse its onslaught.
When caught in the jaws of this enemy,
even this body must be left behind
in a bed still warm and cozy,
with no time even for a parting glance
to possessions, friends, and family.

All duties—supporting friends and attacking foes,
the strivings of a busy life,
you have to leave them all unfinished,
carrying only your karma to the world beyond.

When the difficult, alien pass of *bardo*
is blockaded by the army of the enemy Yama,
then mundane things will let you down;
it's too late then to see their true face.

Dharma is the guide when traveling in an unknown land,
dharma is the provisions when voyaging afar,
dharma is the navigator when negotiating harsh terrain,
so open now the doors of body, speech, and mind to dharma.

Today when fate lies in your hands,
secure a firm grounding in lasting joy,
if not, when your breathing reaches its last,
the time may come when you are totally lost.

Therefore, reflect upon impermanence,
directing your mind to dharma practice—
at all times, beginning, middle, and end—
this is hailed as the path of great light.

When your mind is turned to dharma,
though there are many teachings claiming greatness,
the lineage of Lobsang Victor is supreme—
the quintessential teaching of all the Buddhas.

Strive to imprint within your mind
the unified path of sutra and tantra—
its nature, its levels, its ordered process,
complete, unmistaken—by daily engagement.

Make meditation your principal practice,
pursuing the preliminary and concluding stages
following the advice of the supreme guru,
to give meaning to our human life.

By the positive force of virtuous conduct
destroy the robber, our grasping at permanence,
with its army, the illusion that the world is real.
May we attain the deathless realm!

Movements of Dancing Lightning

Chone Lama Rinpoche (b. 1816)

Father Shepa Dorje, you who fulfill the wishes
of beings infinite as space through the illusory magic
of the inner, outer, and secret deeds;
I place your foot in my heart, the jewel granting all wishes.

Though mountains and valleys of the mind
are oppressed by the darkness of permanence-grasping,
colliding temperatures caused by diverse conditions
give rise to the lightning flashes of these changing thoughts:

In a garden filled with blossoming trees
sway flowers of beautiful color and shape;
in the heat and cold of day and night,
gradually they lose their glow.
This reminds me how unreliable
is our illusory, fragile body
when assaulted by disease.
What benefit is one's family?
Place your hope in the mandala gods, the unfailing family.

From the southern sky thick clouds emerge;
constantly they move: they cannot stay still.
As they begin to throw down the rain,
a powerful storm breaks to disperse them.
This reminds me that my transient body
will soon be destroyed by the clashing of the elements.

What benefit are one's friends?
Depend on your good karma, the sole reliable friend.

In the lush forests around difficult passes,
atop the fruit trees in full bloom,
sweet fruits are ripe, so delicious in taste,
though not for long before they fall.
This reminds me that whoever is born
is taken at the end by death.
What use is wealth?
In your heart hoard learning, the inexhaustible wealth.

From the tip of the high mountain in the east
the blazing sun shines brilliantly;
yet without even a moment to pause
it travels toward the mountain in the west.
This saddens me as it reminds me
that from the moment of my birth
I walk ever closer to my death.
What need have we of leaders?
Follow the injunctions of the compassionate sage.

From the throat of the rocky mountain in the north
begins the descent of a clear stream;
ripples flow one after another
as it moves toward the open sea.
This saddens me as it reminds me
how breath follows breath only to cease.
What use are servants?
Rely on faith, vigor, and wisdom, your loyal servants.

The buzzing of the maiden bees robs the ear's peace
as the autumn season nears its end;

when the harsh winter comes
they are nowhere to be seen.
This saddens me as it reminds me
that the strings of the fiddle
in my throat will one day snap.
What use is fame?
Can its voice be heard in infinite space?

In summer the turquoise dragon throws his lightning noose
and thunders his great voice over distant skies;
he causes fear and threatens hail,
yet in winter he is nowhere heard.
This brings to mind that all will die
who compete for power
from stubborn ego and aggression.
What benefit is high estate?
Seek Buddhahood, the highest state.

Family members whom you've known for long,
disciples nurtured through a teaching life,
when they turn to worldly wealth,
they repay your kindness the wrong way.
This brings to mind the fear
that mind too will part from body, its longtime friend.
What use are this life's friends?
Turn to the ever-present breath, the unfailing friend.

We make complex future plans
with the thought of living long,
yet we see displays of merchandise for sale
labeled "the former owner's dead,"
as if he were struck by a thunderbolt.

This brings to mind the uncertainty:
might I not die this very night?
What point is there in tomorrow's thought?
Tragic will it be if I'm reborn in hell!

In this ghost town of a samsaric realm
illusory beings reap the fruits of karmic deeds,
which though unreal feel tangible,
like experiences in a dream.

May the youthful *rikpa* of my natural mind
unite with the beautiful woman, emptiness,
in a bond never to be parted again.
How I seek to be nurtured by eternal bliss!

I who have turned my mind to dharma this once—
may I sustain this noble way for long;
freed from the bonds of mundane attachment,
may the great ocean of rebirth run dry.

A Word-Brush Drawing of the Monster-Form of Impermanence on Mind's Stone Tablet

Chone Lama Rinpoche (b. 1816)

Your body, union of appearance and emptiness, is an ocean
    cloud;
your speech, union of sound and emptiness, is a scripture
    treasure;
your mind, union of bliss and emptiness, is a mine of
    wisdom and compassion;
O my guru, one with the deity, I invoke you in my heart.

Atop the swaying tree of the transient body
plays the ever-moving mind's little bird;
singing with its unreal voice—
in a sound almost too faint to hear.

Inside the derelict body-guesthouse of four impure elements,
a traveling visitor, the luminous mind, rests for the night;
how can we be certain that this building will not crumble
before the three watches of night are passed?

In the tight and windy gorges of the nostrils
runs the restless mouse, my breath;
Will the cat of illness catch it soon?
Plagued by such fear, restlessly I worry.

Around the mountain of flesh, bones, and blood
hover clouds of fear strangling my life;

Will the sudden storm of perturbed elements
vanish me utterly away?

In the unobstructed sky of the three realms
is impermanence, the eye that oversees all beings;
no one exists who is not driven at the end,
by the karmic storm, to death's mountain in the west.

"When will I be led to the master of fate
by the messenger of clashing elements,
never to be released again?"
This thought grips endlessly my heart.

The uncertain flame of life's butter lamp,
attacked by the winds of fatal conditions,
flickers today so fast—not pausing for an instant;
it's a miracle that it's still burning now!

While looking at other people's deaths,
yet never thinking that we too may die,
we humans are more foolish than animals.
What assurance have we that we won't die tonight?

In the rainbow house of transient life
dances the fickle woman, the lightning flash.
Though your fame resound as loud as thunder;
before long, all will vanish into void.

Poverty closes the chapter of wealth;
old age destroys the glow of youth;
downfall is the result of climbing high;
even friendships end in enmity.

In this illusory town of a samsaric realm,
on the poison tree of the deluded mind
hangs the waste bag of an impure body
tightly tied with ropes of karma and defilement.

The monstrous pig that clings to this as his
has entered my heart through my bones;
it sends a cock and a snake—attachment and hate:
together they cast the spells of destruction.

In life's ocean of mental formations
the powerful tides of pain increase,
creating bubbles of change on the shore;
everything flows in suffering's stream.

Whatever joys there are in the world,
there is nothing that fails to let you down;
dharma alone is ever a friend:
drive home this point to your very heart.

In this vast sea of samsaric arising,
run wild the beings of six realms,
all wailing, all caught in the tides of confusion,
of birth, old age, of sickness and death.
Plant the wish to free them in the depth of your heart.

It's too difficult to turn into a sweet taste
this eternal tree of my mind,
coated with the bitter juice of defilements.
What can a few drops of water do now?

The armor of forbearance, therefore, put on,
the bow of vigor and enthusiasm

and the sharp arrows of diligence, take up.
To conquer the enemy of defilement, aspire.

May the wind of analysis probing the real
lift from the sky, primordially void,
the clouds of ignorance obscuring my mind,
and may the glorious sun of omniscience shine.

Inspire Me to Remember Death

Kelsang Gyatso, seventh Dalai Lama (1708–1757)

Guru, god of gods, my refuge,
my father, the thought of you
alone dispels pain.
As I implore you,
inspire me to remember death,
that I perform a pure dharma practice.

A golden hill ablaze with yellow grass—
silver mists hover round it like a belt;
now it's here, now it's not.
This brings to mind impermanence.

In monsoon summers of heat and heavy rain,
the turquoise fields of wheat heads sway,
by autumn they are desolate.
This brings to mind impermanence.

Ripe fruits weigh down the summer trees;
By wintertime, not one remains,
for all has fallen to the ground.
This brings to mind impermanence.

From atop the towering mountain of the east,
brilliant, spreads the umbrella of the sun;
it does not stay, for it journeys to the west.
This brings to mind impermanence.

Young men and women in their prime,
yesterday, today, and always, die;
prayers for their freedom and rebirth are
    ceaselessly heard.
This brings to mind impermanence.

Thick clouds cast the sky dense gray,
pregnant with rain ready to be dropped;
a powerful gale scatters them.
This brings to mind impermanence.

Amid the glory of a spacious plain
are dotted tents of travelers colorful as the stars;
tomorrow, will only twigs and straw remain.
This brings to mind impermanence.

Nature blooms in the summer's heat;
as I relax enjoying this,
the first chill winds of winter make me sad.
This brings to mind impermanence.

The turquoise dragon of thunder high above,
and doves who sing melodiously below,
suddenly not one of them is found!
This brings to mind impermanence.

Once there lived many holy men
whose dharma medicine cured human ills;
today they watch us from the heavenly realms.
This brings to mind impermanence.

Our parents who gave us birth, and friends
and family so hard to part, will pass away:

the bonds of closeness remain no more.
This brings to mind impermanence.

Arrogant youth full of future schemes,
meticulously planning the next months and years,
is nowhere to be seen; how many loose ends!
This brings to mind impermanence.

Though the immortal diamond body was attained,
even the Buddha too, our refuge, passed away;
our carcass of flesh and blood encased in skin
is bound to perish, like foam on the water's surface.

When grown parents bury a child
who dies immediately after birth,
I too have given up all hope
of an aged death, though I am young.

My body strong and mind fierce,
I tend my friends, combat my enemies;
how can it be that come the wintertime,
my corpse will feast the dogs,
and vultures of the charnel ground will dine?

All human beings whom we see today,
live no more than a hundred years at most;
hardly have I seen one older than this
for each and every one is born to die.

When you look with a clear mind,
everything in the world everywhere

displays the instant dynamism of change.
They all are teachers of impermanence.

My body grown from childhood showed
agility and strength; in old age
when I look now at its parts,
they're my own but too ugly to behold.

Feelings of joy and pain recur,
thoughts of vice and virtue fluctuate,
and attitudes of indifference arise too.
My mind is transient with changing swings.

When I look at my own and others' lives,
it disturbs me that they flicker like a lightning flash.
The harbingers of death surround us all;
what good can I do if I survive at all?

Though the picture of samsara is bright—
family, friends, home, wealth, and everything—
the mind becomes impeded by its ties;
but this illusion will disappear one day!

The body moves on its last bed,
last words are spoken in a slurred way,
last thoughts occur in a clouded mind.
When will this moment come for me?

My past was full of negative acts;
I'm poor in merit for my next rebirth;
I've no idea where I'll be going;
when I think of dying, I am afraid.

Therefore, I myself and everyone like me,
should not be beset by trivial chores.
Appeal to guru, deity, and *dakini*
to be with us when our roll call comes.

It's vital to form the state of mind
to die with confidence and joy
with a heart imbued by white karma's light.
Be grounded in sutra and tantra's depth.

By partaking in this discourse
may I and those like me—
mind-hardened even toward dharma—
be moved toward renunciation;
with open spirit, may we be free.

Ramblings of an Aged Man

Gungthang Tenpai Drönme (1762–1822)

I

I bow to you, enlightened ones,
who have conquered age and death,
for you've destroyed the seeds of birth.
Cut the ties of life and death!

Once a withered, aged man
was lying on life's empty plain;
a young man haughty in his youth
came and said the following lines:

"Old man, how come you are so slow
in all your doings, getting up,
walking, sitting down; why so
unlike others?" The old man replied:

"Listen to me, O young man,
blooming, flying, in your prime,
I was like you, nay, better, once,
and only a few years ago.

"I caught wild horses when I ran,
I tamed the wild yaks of the north,
I rivaled the soaring of the birds,
my beauty challenged all the gods!

"I wore gorgeous costly cloth,
I adorned myself with precious jewels,

I ate the best, delicious food,
I rode fast-charging thoroughbreds.

"There isn't a sport I haven't tried;
there isn't a joy I haven't known;
never came the thought of death;
I knew not that old age would strike.

"As I was busy with bustling life
midst friends and many relatives,
the deceptive suffering of old age came.
Unannounced, it struck me down.

"I didn't perceive my own aging,
when I did it was too late;
I see myself in the mirror now,
I am disgusted by my face!

"Body and mind are weakening,
it all declines from the head down;
the ritual waters of aging
are sprinkled from the crown!

"My hair's conch white, but not because
all filth is washed; the spraying
spit of the lord of death
has fallen on me like a mist!

"The furrows on my forehead
are not the folds of a newborn child,
they're the lines notched up by Messenger Time
for all the years that have gone by.

"The constant blinking of my eyes,
not caused by irritating smoke,
is due to obscuring cataracts
causing loss of sight; I can't help it!

"Stretching out my eager ears
is not because I hope to hear
a secret, but to hear at all;
for all sounds echo from afar.

"The constant dripping from my nose
is not a garland of woven pearls!
It's the melting of youth's block of ice
by the piercing rays of the raging sun.

"Dropping my coronet of teeth
is not to change for new, fresh ones;
it's the cracking of old instruments
as my eating time is near its end.

"My constant saliva spray
aims not to moisten the soil;
I am spitting with revulsion
at what I sought with joy.

"My speaking in a halting way—
not because it's foreign speech—
but rather that my tongue is tired
by excessive indulgence in senseless speech.

"This ugly face of puckered lines
is not a monkey mask I wear;

the borrowed youth is taken away.
My true face is revealed!

"The endless shaking of my head
is not that I am jeering,
but uncontrolled the juddering skull
as I am struck by Yama's club.

"My stooping low when walking,
not searching for a needle lost,
but the condition of an aged man
who's lost his youth, his memory.

"My crouching on all fours is not
because I'm aping animals,
but my arms must assist:
my legs cannot support the weight.

"My slumping when I try to sit
aims not to annoy my friends,
but my body has lost its link
with the joyful play of mind.

"The slowness of my dithering steps—
not an important person's walk—
is aging's unbalanced lurch
burdened by decrepitude.

"The constant waving of my hands—
not greed's grabbing for more wealth—
is caused by fear that from my palms
all will be snatched by Yama.

"Taking little food and drink
is due not to miserliness;
it's because digestion's gone.
The old man's afraid of falling down.

"Wearing light and easy clothes
is not that I am fashionable.
For even clothes have become a weight
as I have lost my body's strength.

"Gasping for breath with a tight chest,
I am not blowing mantras to others.
It's the early sign of vanishing life
exhaling into thin air.

"These changes in my behavior
are not just absence of care;
I am possessed by the devil of age.
My self-control is nowhere.

"The forgetting of tasks—not proud
negligence—is mental demise,
as memory fails, mindfulness
falls off, the senses collapse.

"Young man, don't disparage me,
old age is there for all;
in three years, even you will see
its early messengers come.

"You may not like what I have said,
but this will be your fate;

as life spans become shorter now
you may not reach my age.
Even if you do, you might
be inarticulate."

2

Hearing this, the young man said:
"Better death by far than living
a traitor, like you, despised by men,
even the dogs' plaything."

The old man smiled and replied:
"It's fools who wish to live long
yet cannot accept old age.
What joy is there in dying?

"He who has not abused others' gifts,
has observed the precepts profoundly,
has studied, reflected, meditated,
might reap some joy in dying.

"As I cannot recall having pursued
any of these instructions,
though old, I prefer to remain alive,
even but for an extra day."

3

This caused the youth a change of heart.
"You are right, old man," replied he.
"What I can see with my naked eyes
fits well with your description.

What you have said has affected me.
The pain of age is tragic.
Old man, you are wise.
If there is anything that can stop this pain,
do tell me frankly."

The old man smiled and replied:
"There *is* a solution. It's simple.
You need not do much.
What is born must die;
few reach old age before dying.

"Though what you seek is freedom from death,
this cannot be found anywhere.
Buddhas, bodhisattvas, great men, and kings
have perished, everywhere dying.

"All those living too will die.
Can you alone survive them?
Practice dharma, O young man:
though age will weaken your body,
you can arouse joy in the mind.
So even when death strikes you,
you'll be like a boy coming home.
A way more effective than this one
even the Buddha could not find.
This is my heart's testament.
What I say may be hearsay;
seek what is best for your interest."

4

"Okay, Okay," replied the youth.
"But my family commitments

and endless obligations
leave many loose ends.
I have no time for years.
After this, I'll certainly pursue
the dharma. Shall we meet again?"

Dejected, the old man shot back:
"What you say is utter nonsense.
I too once thought, 'I shall pursue
the practice of the dharma,
but I have no time for years.'
Loose ends are like an old man's mustache,
the more it's shaved the more it grows.

"Before your 'few years' pass, life's end
may come. Procrastination
fools everyone; you have no hope
of practicing the dharma.
Why do you waste my time, young man,
with empty words? Go home and leave
this aged man to mutter OM MANI PADME HUM."

5

This shocked the youth. "Old man,
don't make such rash and thoughtless comments.
How can a man leave everything—
all tasks and obligations?"

The old man laughed, "Ha! Ha!
It's easy to say this to me;
but there's a stern old man down south

who doesn't care for your loose ends.
See if you can talk to him.
When he pounces suddenly,
everyone departs.
Old or young, high or low,
they die immediately.
And all loose ends are abruptly cut.
Then you've no choice but to leave;
the laws of nature never fail.
Since loose ends must anyway
be cut, why not do it now,
when it is meaningful?
Few are they who speak with real benefit,
fewer still are those who hear their speech!"

6

The youth bowed to the man and cried:
"Even lamas with swirling parasols
and learned Geshes of great fame
have no teaching more profound than this.
O master in old man's disguise,
I'll follow exactly as advised;
please give me more advice."

The old man said, "Okay, okay!
This old man has experienced much.
Nothing is harder than to secure
a base in dharma practice.
When you are old and withered,
this cannot be achieved;
so strive when you are young.

"If you secure the base in youth,
in age it comes more easily.
If you fully penetrate the essence of the teachings,
all you do becomes dharma.

"Nurture not too many thoughts,
focus the mind on dharma.
Seek the root, the guru's guidance;
guard the precepts as you would your eyes;
root out all mundane concerns.

"Study, reflect, and meditate,
the essence of Lobsang Victor's path.
Endeavor in the practices—
avoidance and affirmation—
enlightenment is at your fingertips!

"At times I feel joyful, at times, grateful.
O dear son, may your wishes be fulfilled."
To this assented both of them. And from that very day,
the young man practiced dharma
free of the four paired worldly stains.

7

May this song on the discourse
of an old man and a youth
inspire myself and others
toward dharma practice.

Though I am myself not realized,
yet as the minds of beings are diverse
perhaps this too will benefit some.
Therefore I, Könchok Drönme, have written it.

Yearning
for Solitude

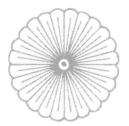

The Red Rocky Mountain

Milarepa (1040–1123)

This lonely mountain, a place of solitude,
the ground where the Buddhas found enlightenment,
the home of great mystics in the past,
is the spot where I—the only human—dwell.

This red rocky mountain with a jeweled valley
is Garuda's fortress, crowned by clouds from the south;
below is a snakelike flowing river,
and the vultures hover in between.
The plants weave a canopy of leafy nets,
the trees sway in the dancing breeze.
Bees are chanting with music and song,
the fragrance of flowers pervades the air.
Birdsong resounds in melody.

In this red rocky mountain with a jeweled valley,
sparrows test their fledgling wings,
monkeys practice their agile skills,
beasts extend their stamina to sprint.
I, Milarepa, train in meditation:
to develop the experience of the two *bodhi* minds.
The local spirit and I are in harmony:
O spirits, invisible forces gathered here,
drink this nectar of love and compassion
and depart to your own abodes.

The Joys of the Solitary Hills

Kalden Gyatso (1607–1677)

I pray to Tenpai Gyaltsen, savior of beings,
royal ruler of Tsongkhapa's spiritual realm.
I pray, help me realize the profound way.

Due to your kindness, O protector,
I have entered the Buddha's gate,
and have engaged in extensive learning,
have taught assemblies of learned scholars
ways of the teaching that I have learned.

But now, let me follow in your footsteps
and seek the joy of a solitary grove.
In the past, I led a life of worldly delusion
under the spell of material gain.

Now, let me be free of these entrapments,
let me, Kalden Gyatso, go to the solitary hills.
In the past I roamed in all directions—
to find myself a fraud.

Now, let me join the ranks of the wise,
let me, Kalden, born in Rong, go to the solitary hills.
Because my mind was far from the tranquil dharma way,
today it is still unsoaked by wisdom, as a stone in water.

Now, that my mind be attuned to the dharma,
Kalden today seeks the solitary hills.

O monks, village elders, and donors,
turn your hearts toward the dharma and be in joy.

I, Kalden, shall go without looking back
to the joy of a solitary grove.
Listen youths, you who have joined the order,
depart for the central land now,
and exert yourselves in profound spiritual learning.

But I will go the hills without hesitation.
Those who are too young to travel so far,
yet aspire to attain great learning,
go to the nearby centers of learning in Do-me.
But I will go to the faraway hills.

O my disciples, you who have entrusted your care to me,
from now, seek refuge in the Three Jewels.
Strive to realize the stainless teaching.
But I will go to the solitary hills.

As a cuckoo flies to faraway lands with an ear of corn in her beak,
so I shall travel swiftly to the distant hills,
contented with only my learning as my provision bag.
As the eagle flies higher and higher in heaven
to whatsoever height she desires,
I shall go farther and farther from home
to the joys of a solitary grove.

A Song by a Yogi in Solitude

Shapkar Tsogdruk Rangdröl (1781–1851)

Free indeed is the yogi
who lives everywhere with abandon:
in cave houses atop mountains,
in the shade of blossoming trees,
in a hut amid the open fields,
in a small white cotton tent.

I will sing from afar
a song of joy and peace:

Because of you, O guru, most sublime and wise,
whose kindness surpasses even the Buddha's,
I *understand* the truth:
that all events and happenings—
the union of form and emptiness—
are nothing but the play of mind.

Mysterious, incomprehensible,
I realize, is my mind—
the root of prison and freedom,
ungraspable, without substance.

Living in solitude I place my mind
with natural ease upon suchness—
this mind, as light as a wisp of cotton fluff.
The darkness of unknowing
recedes at its own pace,

and the vast sky of the infinite real
wakes with the light of dawn.

"Whether it *is* or it is *not*"—
doubts engendered by skepticism—
are qualms with no significance,
questions the Buddhas wouldn't answer.

Oh, the great congregation:
yogis of *mahamudra*, famed and wise,
who see the naked face of the real,
while residing atop Tsari Mountain,
a heavenly realm, true abode of dakinis,
where all mystic events flow spontaneous.

Oh, enter the four features
of *dharmakaya*—the Reality Essence:
empty as space, brilliant as sun,
transparent as mirror, sharp as eyes.

Let us then travel together
to the realm of the real itself.
As the discourse of philosophers,
conducted by all-knowing scholars
in the debating courtyards,
is a melodious tune to the ear,
so too are songs of experience
sung in solitude by yogis
who have entered the Great Oneness—
mahamudra and Zokpa Chenpo.

Longing for the Mountains of Solitude

Za Paltrül Rinpoche (1808–1887)

Fooled in samsara town—
the endless cycle of countless chores,
preoccupations of a delusory world—
this boy's mind longs for mountains of solitude.

Hassled by monastery life—
the hustle of duties and communal dues,
pursuits of pointless distraction—
This boy's mind longs for mountains of solitude.

Whomever I look at, I see at death's threshold;
whatever I think on, I sense denial of dying,
grasping at the deathless; in this courtyard of death,
this boy's mind longs for mountains of solitude.

Whomever I meet with manifests clinging and repulsion;
whomever I talk to brings deception and lies;
faced by companions without virtuous conduct,
this boy's mind longs for mountains of solitude.

Behold, beings in the three realms are fooled by afflictions;
the beings of the six realms are led astray;
delusion engenders the birth of suffering for all;
this boy's mind longs for mountains of solitude.

By the blessings of the undeceiving guru and the
    [Three] Jewels,

may I attain and persevere in solitude;
by the force of a place of seclusion,
may I attain a mystic's isolation
of body, speech, and mind.
May I be blessed by the mountains of solitude.

Calling the
Guru from Afar

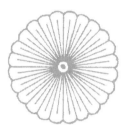

A Beggar and His Guru

Milarepa (1040–1123)

To see my father guru's face and hear his voice
transforms this beggar's grief into a mystic's revelation.
Recalling my teacher's exemplary life,
reverence dawns deep in my heart.

Blessings and kindness directly enter me;
all perceptions of nonvirtue come to cease.
Though this song of lament—remembering you—
might annoy you, O my guru,
sorrow is this beggar's fate;
I'll still grieve. Sustain me with your kindness.

Asceticism born of heartfelt perseverance
is my service to please you, O my father guru.
Wandering in the wilderness alone
is my service to please the dakinis.

The pursuit of dharma without self-regard
is my service to the teachings of the Buddha.
The union of life and meditation
is my gift to fellow beings without a savior.

To persevere through life—its happiness and sorrow—
is the broom that sweeps away our karma and afflictions.
The fortitude of abstaining from the food of pollution
is the basis for transcendent realization.

I shall repay my teacher's kindness through repeated
    meditation;
Nurture me with kindness, O supreme guru!
Bless me, that this beggar succeed in his hermit's
    isolation.

May I See My Guru Again and Again

Natsok Rangdröl (b. 1608)

The compassionate guru
attracts disciples who respect him.
Let's receive his profound instruction.

Though we cannot be together at all times,
May the guru's deeds flourish;
and may the disciples' realizations be enhanced.
At this auspicious, solitary place,
always with a sense of increasing fortune,
may I see my guru again and again.

The sky—so wide and vast—the clear,
radiant sun and moon, together bring
powerful illumination. Though they cannot stay
together at once, the bright sky and
the unobscured sun and moon roam
about the four continents, dispelling darkness.
May I see my guru again and again.

A flower, colorful and robust,
attracts bees that hover humming songs.
Though they cannot remain together long,
if the flower is not destroyed by pests
and the bees not chased away by hailstorms,
the bees can sing and drink the flowers' hearts.
May I see my guru again and again.

On branching trees covered with leaves
cuckoos sing melodious tunes.
They drink the raindrops and eat the fruits,
though they cannot be together long.
If the maiden tree is not cut down
and the cuckoos return from far-off lands,
they can drink the drops and feast on the fruits.
May I see my guru again and again.

The mountains, lush and spacious,
attract the roaming creatures of the wild.
They eat the grasses and race each other in the shade.
Though they cannot be together all the time—
may there be no landslides on the mountainside,
and may no hunters shoot the animals for game.
May I see my guru again and again.

The guru who is master of instruction
attracts devotees with good resources.
They seek wisdom and sing in admiration,
though they cannot be together at all times.
May the guru live long and the devotees
enjoy good health. In such auspiciousness
may they meet again and again.

This hermitage of Karma Lhalong
attracts great practitioners, with great realizations,
who sing their experience as they meditate.
That this be always so, may the gurus
enjoy good health, and may their practices flourish
at this site, where the welfare of self and others is fulfilled.
May all of us meet again and again.

A Song of Desolation

Kalden Gyatso (1607–1677)

How joyful it would be if my guru Tenzin Lobsang were alive!
How happy I would be to receive instructions from him at will!
How cheerful it would be if I could see his face, radiant like the
    moon!
How blissful I would be to drink his discourse, richer than nectar!

Only by your kindness, O protector,
the sun of learning and practice, the Buddha's teachings,
shines forth in this distant land of Amdo.
What has entered the heart of those who recall not your kindness?

Now that you have left this place
to depart to the pure realm of the Buddhas,
I cannot find a guru, despite repeated searching,
in whom to entrust my wholehearted well-being.

Behold me, I appeal to you night and day,
my heart filled with reverence and sadness,
remembering your enlightened form;
pray cast on me your compassionate gaze.

It is as rare as seeing a daytime star
to find a teacher who is possessed
of even part of your qualities,
let alone one endowed with all.

What point is there if I remain alive?
I have lost all hope for the dharma.
Conceit rules the world.
O guru, at this time, grant me your compassion.

On the Death of
Kyabje Trijhang Rinpoche, 1982

Zemey Lobsang Palden (1927–1996)

O mine of compassion, my father,
the mere thought of you relieves our pain;
O glorious Vajradhara, accomplished in the great union,
you are the cloud, showering dharma nectar.
I recall you, O my refuge, from depths of my heart.
Pray sustain us!

Tragic is your sudden departure:
you have left for the pure realms of the *yoginis*
via the silken path prepared by myriads of dakinis,
amid a rainbow canopy of color.

O my refuge, the glorious father, free of faults,
you may delight upon the celestial throne
midst countless tantra-practicing disciples
who are entranced by the music of dancing bells;
but can you bear to abandon your children,
entrapped in this barren gorge of terror,
enveloped by the darkness, all-obscure,
of ignorance, tortured by the fruits of past deeds?

Though we haven't forgotten your diamond words:
"Tame your mind, obstructions will diminish,"
heard when we drank the nectar of your presence,
yet the strength of our endeavor remains weak.

The dazzling cloud of your enlightened form
dancing within the eternal space of dharmakaya
is today no more: it has vanished into the expanse.
To whom shall we now turn for dharma rain?

The brilliant sun, the all-encompassing umbrella,
the friend who opens the petals of the heart's lotus,
today lies sleeping with the gods of the west.
To whom shall we now turn to unfold *our* hearts' lotus?

The translucent moon free of all blemish,
perfect in its attributes and brilliance,
today it is threatened by Rahula's eclipse.
To whom shall we turn now for cool blessings?

The wish-granting tree resplendent with branches
of virtue and insight, replete with fruits of goodness,
has today been felled by a storm.
To whom shall we turn now for fulfillment?

The majestic form whose mere sight liberates,
Mount Kailash, Buddha's emanation,
is today melted by the pollution of a degenerate age.
To whom shall we turn now for instruction's flowing river?

I wonder if my father guru hears these
lamenting sounds of my plea.
I wonder if my father guru sees this
prostrated disciple distraught.

I wonder if my father guru knows this
desperate fate of an orphan.

I wonder if my father guru feels pity for this
piercing pain like a sharp thorn within.

May this lamentation of an abandoned child—
sung with the cries of despairing grief,
crazed at heart and lost of mind—
reach the ears of my father guru.

Pray take us your children, your disciples,
after you to the dakinis' pure abode,
the realm where my father guru now resides;
nurture us with the nectar of your words.

Today the essential teachings of the ear-whispered lineage
of Tsongkhapa are like the setting sun atop the western
    mountain;
they are threatened by the twilight of an immoral path.
Can you, O father guru, bear to see this lineage obscured?

Swiftly show us the face of reincarnation
who'll take up your mantle, O father guru.
Pray be our heroic guide
leading beings toward freedom.

That these aspirations be realized,
may the gurus, deities, and dakinis
and the powerful protectors of the dharma
sustain us by the force of their power.

May all of us and those related to us
soon behold your noble face.
By seeing it, may we traverse the ladder of the path
and attain the supreme state of the four *kayas*.

Echoes
of Emptiness

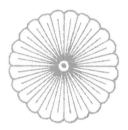

Reflections on Emptiness

Tsongkhapa (1357–1419)

Existence and extinction are primordially equal,
for all conceptions—even birth and death—have ceased.
This spacelike nature is free of all limits—
devoid of characteristics grasped by the mind.

All conditions, all dependence, are but labels of mind;
mind too is empty of its own being.
Thus, through relations of mutual dependence,
samsara and nirvana are differentiated.

Except by virtue of the mind's fantasies,
there is nothing that exists in its own right;
being and nothingness, birth and death, good and evil—
these polarities too are products of mind.

The paths of delusion and enlightenment
being by nature empty of their own being,
how can there be a path
to eradicate evil and enhance its antidotes?

Not even an atom of matter can be found,
for all things are like the waters of mirage;
the wise discuss the dependent origination
to counter the fears of minds steeped in grasping.

To the wise, free of views and opinions,
even permanence and impermanence are alien notions;

for if the son of a barren woman does not exist,
how can there be his birth and death?

Since nothing exists as it is imagined,
all things are empty as perceived.
Since even the void appears,
it appears without existence.
Wise is the one who sees this difficult path;
profound is the path realized by the wise.
What is perceived by the wise
exists as the wise have perceived it;
wise is the one who perceives
suchness—the way things exist.
Ignorant are the deluded, for they falsely perceive;
those who falsely perceive are fools.
He who clings through grasping,
swiftly, swiftly he turns in the round of existence.

In Praise of the Vision of Father Lobsang

Kelsang Gyatso, seventh Dalai Lama (1708–1757)

At the center of my heart,
the eight-petaled lotus dances
the dance of diamond mind,
born of the changeless ground.
O father Lobsang Drakpa,
incarnate form of all the Buddhas,
I salute you, father guru.

All samsara and nirvana,
grounds of being, without exception,
are but constructs of the mind;
mind too is birthless, deathless,
when searched by a penetrating probe.
Emaho! *This* is the nature,
the essence of true being.

As clouds clear from the autumn sky,
all dual perception and experience
cease within the union of space and mind.
I, a yogin of unborn space,
behold the spectacle of great illusion—
the wondrous lies of the void,
ungrounded in any way.

In this ecstatic marriage
of appearance and emptiness,
restored is my faith in dependent origination,
which is illusory yet infallible.

By the eloquent words of father Lobsang,
himself the supreme Wisdom Treasure,
and the kindness of my perfect teachers,
I have sung this song of ultimate meaning.

Ramblings of a Drunken Bee

Chone Lama Rinpoche (b. 1816)

This orange heap of radiant light—
the dancing form of the innate mind,
in the chakra chamber of my heart—
my father guru, I ever seek you.

Bless me, help me penetrate the depth—
not merely in concepts and images—
the Middle Way, union of appearance and emptiness,
transcending the bounds of permanence and nothingness.

I delight in singing this song,
as if repeating the content of a teaching
uttered in a voice of perfect eloquence
by the glorious tongue of the supreme sage.

Constellations of myriad celestial bodies
appear bright in the night's dark sky,
yet in the brilliant rays of the sun by day
all perish in the sphere of voidness.

This appearance—the world of dependent aggregations—
seemingly tangible to the deluded mind,
when probed by the question "What is real?"
offers nothing to withstand the search.

To the eye afflicted by cataracts,
empty space seems filled with falling hair;

when treated with medicine and cured,
clear sight returns unobscured.

To the mind deceived by demons grasping at the real,
though phenomena of every sort appear,
they are absent when insight probes reality itself
and sees through the mind's grand deception.

Light is devoid of its own being
inside a butter lamp's hollow space,
yet when oil, wick, and fire coincide,
a flame that can burn comes to life!

All things occurring and known to occur,
all samsara and nirvana, are empty.
Yet who can deny how vivid and diverse,
are the rough sketches of our thoughts?

The illusion of repulsive and attractive forms
can cause fear, lust, and anger within;
yet no benefit nor harm exists
in the realm of the ultimate truth.

With the friends and enemies of the world,
a restless mind is plagued by hope and apprehension;
this misery is born of holding real all things
that appear to be solid, yet are empty.

The glistening, tiny dewdrop
at the tip of a blade of grass—
it is natural that it evaporates
in even the gentlest warmth of the sun.

In all things codependent,
right from the very moment of their birth,
the seed of destruction lies inherent;
their end requires no other cause.

In lakes and ponds where waters gather,
attacked by heavy-beating rains,
the banks give way, the torrent gushes out;
the cause is water's fluid nature.

In this prison of the three realms
bound by chains of karma and delusion,
whatever feelings arise of joy or pain—
all are states of samsaric suffering.

In a dream created by a mind asleep,
no matter how long we enjoy the phantom
prosperities of worldly wealth,
only an emptiness lingers when we wake.

Wealth, house, and friends,
acquired with great effort and will—
all that life's offered to enjoy—
today nothing remains but a memory.

A flash of lightning, stark
against the sky, disappears;
where does it come from, where does it go?
Does it remain? How can we tell?

What is vivid to us now,
this spectacle of objects—so many and so real—

when examined with a discerning mind,
loses tangibility; for all are devoid of ground!

By the contingent power of rain,
falling from the floating canopy of clouds,
from an empty space free of obstructions,
fruits ripen, crops grow upon the ground.

From multiple, interacting causes and conditions
in the empty space of the radiant mind,
fruits diverse both pure and impure
arise as sentient beings and their world.

Though lacking in perfect inner absorption,
spontaneously I sing a melodious tune
the experiential music reflecting in words—
the true fruit of learning the scriptures of the Middle Way.

By the virtue of uttering these words,
may all the beings, who have been my mother,
discern the middle path, so hard to see,
in accord with the Buddha's great intent.

A Response to a Logician

Milarepa (1040–1123)

I bow at the feet of my teacher Marpa.
And sing this song in response to you.
Listen, pay heed to what I say,
forget your critique for a while.

The best seeing is the way of "nonseeing"—
the radiance of mind itself.
The best prize is what cannot be looked for—
the priceless treasure of mind itself.

The most nourishing food is "noneating"—
the transcendent food of *samadhi*.
The most thirst-quenching drink is "nondrinking"—
the nectar of heartfelt compassion.

Oh, this self-realizing awareness
is beyond words and description!
This mind is not of the world of children,
nor is it that of logicians.

Attaining the truth of "nonattainment,"
you receive the highest initiation.
Perceiving the void of high and low,
you reach the sublime stage.

Approaching the truth of "nonmovement,"
you follow the supreme path.

Knowing the end of birth and death,
the ultimate purpose is fulfilled.

Seeing the emptiness of reason,
supreme logic is perfected.
When you know that great and small are groundless,
you have entered the highest gateway.

Comprehending beyond good and evil
opens the way to perfect skill.
Experiencing the dissolution of duality,
you embrace the highest view.

Observing the truth of "nonobservation"
opens the way to meditating.
Comprehending beyond "ought" and "oughtn't"
opens the way to perfect action.

When you realize the truth of "noneffort,"
you are approaching the highest fruition.
Ignorant are those who lack this truth:
arrogant teachers inflated by learning,
scholars bewitched by mere words,
and yogis seduced by prejudice.
For though they yearn for freedom,
they find only enslavement.

A Spontaneous Song Evoked by the Dream-Girl

Chone Lama Rinpoche (b. 1816)

The dance of the indestructible mind,
the blazing orange flame of Manjushri,
this essence of my kind guru,
I treasure you in the lotus of my heart.

Change radically the direction of my mind—
fooled till now by the illusion of the real—
plant in my heart the wisdom eye
that perceives everything as void.

A mind oppressed by sleep
and without the senses active
may enjoy dreams of prosperous success.
When suddenly woken from sleep,
this mind is struck with sadness;
The gap between the experience and the fact
is the true measure of dream objects.

On the surface of a clear pond,
free of any polluting particles,
the moon's reflection shines through
from between curtains of cloud;
yet when you stir the pond bed,
dirt disperses throughout the pool,
and the moon's image disappears.
This is the true face of the moon in water.

On a clean, shiny mirror
free of stains or scratches,
vivid indeed is the face
with darting eyes and quivering lips.
When touched by the hand,
there is no depth but surface only—
void though seemingly real.
This is the true face of reflection.

When you shout aloud
in an empty cave,
it sounds as though someone is replying;
yet the cave is deserted,
there is no one who can respond.
The echoes are void though seemingly real;
this is the true face of an echo.

In the clear and empty sky
free of cloudy obstruction,
vivid indeed is the rainbow,
brilliant and colorful;
when one looks closer,
one cannot grasp it, as it disappears.
This is the true face of a rainbow.

From the space of void's nature
arises the multiplicity of the dependent world;
it's unfailing and distinct,
yet probed with the question "What is real?"
the solidity is no more and disappears into void.
This is the true face of dependent origination.

This short song too
was written on the full moon day
of the eleventh month of the water-tiger year,
recollecting, while awake,
illusions of the dream world,
by a man called Suddhisara,
who has gained some conviction
in the meaning of the great Middle Way.

A Sky with a Center and Borders!

Longchen Rabjampa (1308–1363)

O dharma master, my glorious refuge, pure as sky,
knowing the essence, you are free from samsara and nirvana;
your mind is fused with Samantabhadra's wisdom.
I bow at your feet my guru,
incomparable protector of beings.

In rikpa awareness samsara and nirvana are undistinguished;
in the primordial unborn, the phenomena limit beyond cognition,
there is no dualism of object and subject,
thus the essential rikpa flows unobstructed,
spectacularly vivid and naked!

Whatever appears has no basis. It's an empty form,
like the moon reflected in a pool of water,
which you perceive though it is absent, which seems real
though it is but a nonexistent illusion.
Free of content, the void is vivid and naked!

Self-illuminating, the void is empty of distinctions—
manifestation is a traceless memory in an empty space;
mind and its modalities have no objectivity,
no ground or roots. Object-free,
the subject is thoroughly void!

Whatever appears—samsara and nirvana, container and
        contained—
is in the uncreated, primordial state of voidness.

This self-arisen rikpa, which is groundless
and without base—in this rikpa, all appears
vivid and unobstructed!

Free of all boundaries is the flow of rikpa,
nongrasping, self-illuminating, penetrating essence.
In enlightened thought, all beings
are utterly pure from the beginning: the naked
ever-presence is vivid and beyond cognition!

It does not attend to the way things arise,
it conceives not the forms in which things appear;
in self-liberating rikpa—without creation
and dissolution—the permeation
of effulgent flow is naked and vivid!

Neither external nor withdrawn inward,
the nonengaging concentration is beyond cognition.
Within the inconceivable that is neither meditation
nor the absence of meditation, the self-arisen
rikpa is naked and vivid!

The flow of rikpa—pervasive and unhindered
by intervening stages—is naked self-illumination,
free of all objectifications. In this primordial expanse,
devoid of inner and outer content, unmediated
rikpa is vivid as dharmakaya!

In enlightenment, intent is spontaneous and accomplished,
a spontaneity uncreated at its base;
cause and effect, good and evil, samsara and nirvana,

are nondual; radiant rikpa is vivid
as the body of Buddha's consummate bliss!

Stainless rikpa is unperturbed and unfixed—
nothing is established or obstructed;
in this sphere, free of all extremes
of existence and nonexistence, the source is vivid
as the body of the Buddha incarnate!

Though appearing as samsara it is baseless—
an empty form: there has never been a defilement
of the essence; a clear image of illusion,
undimmable, it points to the vivid
eradication of samsara!

In its totally unobstructed self-effulgence,
whatever may appear—transcendent bodies,
wisdom, or pure realms—is groundless,
empty form; samsara and nirvana
are nameless and vividly empty!

Within rikpa though good and bad appear,
they are merely the unobstructed play
of self-illuminating, clear, and empty rikpa.
It neither moves to others nor is self-established.
The nondual, self-illuminating rikpa is vivid!

Phenomena are but illusory constructs.
In the absence of inner and outer objects,
nowhere to be found, the self-arisen
wisdom is beyond elaboration. At the end of experience,
vivid indeed is the cessation of cognition!

Whether it circles, transcends, appears, or becomes,
grasping, perceiving—all are absent of foundation;
in the Great Perfection, the apex
of all the vehicles, they are originally enlightened
as vivid dharmakaya!

In the sphere of great liberation, free of affirmation
and denial, in the unchanging expanse
of self-arisen rikpa, in the Great Perfection,
which is beyond cognition, everything appears
vividly as all-performing rikpa!

The great expansive ground—unconceived,
unexamined, unstirred from its sphere—sleeps
in its dharmakaya couch; stainless
in its self-cognition, manifest in its great fruition,
self-arisen rikpa is unchanging and vivid!

In the dharmakaya sky, cloudless, clear
of deeds and effort, the power of self-arisen rikpa's
realization crushes the abyss, the vehicles
of cause and effect. The great garuda of rikpa
soars shining originally vivid!

The adamantine essence body, the perfection of great art,
heart of Great Perfection, the apex of all vehicles—
as it manifests in me, Longchen Rabjampa,
I hoist this banner to ensure the freedom of all beings
from the three realms. May all sentient beings,
without exception, be totally freed from all hardships,
and become spontaneously the ever-perfect dharmakaya.

Melodies of an Echo

Chone Lama Rinpoche (b. 1816)

My sole refuge, Ngawang, I honor you with my crown—
touching the jewel of your feet until my enlightenment.
You create and absorb multitudes of mandalas—
wisdom's play that purifies all pollution in the expanse.

As I look at the world of appearance, so solid,
perceived through the delusions of the sixfold consciousness,
who can negate the vividness of our perceptions—
beautiful and ugly, yet devoid of the real?

Attachment arises for the things of beauty,
fear and apprehension for things repulsive;
explore: are beauty and ugliness really there
as grasped by the mind projecting them?

Whatever happiness and joy—the thrill
of samara—relished in the past,
all that which fills your memory,
is it no more than last night's dream?

The end of a pleasure once enjoyed,
transient like the dancing queen of lightning,
is enveloped by the darkness, the pain of change;
what benefit is there in such fleeting joys?

The target of my heart repeatedly is pierced
by arrows adorned with feathers of attraction,

arrows sharpened and propelled by desire,
and shot from the twisted bow of illusion.

The objects of attachment are a barren woman's son,
the mind of desire is roped by turtle's hair,
cut it with a sharp sword of rabbit's horn!
Be cheerful! Why be saddened by nonexistent things?

Enemies and friends are constructs of the mind;
mind itself is constructed on experience and events;
there is nothing that is concrete and rooted,
for all are merely names and labels.

In this great city of ghosts, the residing guests,
illusory beings all, as in a dream,
experience joy and pain in rotating cycles:
though unreal, who can deny this?

These thoughts occurred in my mind one night,
induced by the illusions of my dreams.
They should have stayed in my heart, but they slipped
from the mouth of a man with DHIH in his name.

The Love Dance of Emptiness and Appearance

Chone Lama Rinpoche (b. 1816)

Sustain me, Manjushri, wielder of the blazing sword,
the sharp destroyer of dark ignorance.
Sustain me, by the brilliant sun of wisdom
illuminating the equanimity of all.

My concrete perceptions of a substantial world,
when its true mode of being is sought,
seem unreal and evaporate into the void.
Behold the vivid magic of unprobed form!

Through the wonders of codependent arising,
one sees the shimmering of the moon in a lake;
when you swim there and search for the moon,
nothing is found; the moon disappears.

It is natural to my senses and conception
that an autonomous, substantial "I" appears;
yet when I search the complex of my body and mind,
akin to milk in water, this independent "I" dissolves.

By dint of squeezing my eyeballs,
a double moon appears though there is only one;
yet when I leave my senses undisturbed,
I realize this double moon is an illusion.

When my mind is polluted by grasping at the real,
everything appears to exist in its own right;

yet when probed by the question "What is the real?"
everything I find is the construct of my thoughts.

Obscured by cataracts, the eyes seem to see
the falling of hair in the sky;
when the cataract is removed through surgery,
the illusion of falling hair is revealed.

When I'm drunk by the wine of grasping at the real,
everything goes wrong because the world's conceived
    as solid;
yet when the awareness that dismantles solidity arises,
I'll see the true face of the mind grasping the real.

In the magical meeting of rain, clouds, and sun,
a brilliant rainbow of the five colors appears—
its unmoving ends seem rooted to the ground;
yet as you approach, it runs away and fades.

To the unquestioning, natural mind,
there're only the spectacles of ephemeral things;
yet in the mind's probing into reality,
nothing exists except the ineffable essence.

It's not that nothing exists: there are phenomena,
but nothing is as it seems to the mind;
those who stride the Middle Way free of being
and nonbeing, they are called the Madhyamikas.

The supreme, cooling nirvana peace
does not manifest without meditation;

for knowing the ultimate—as it really is—
dawns from the penetration of dependent arising.

From the aggregations of dependent factors
the self-image of the ultimate is displayed;
and from the ultimate space, free of all duality,
the worlds of form and diversity are born.

When form reveals the content of the void,
and the void makes way for spontaneous appearance,
then you have entered the delight of the sages;
never again to be prey to extreme views.

This poem has been uttered by a man
whose intelligence is not starved of effort,
who is like an ocean never satisfied
in absorbing knowledge of the vast scriptures
and reflecting on their wonderful meanings.

Awake from the Slumber of Ignorance!

Kelsang Gyatso, seventh Dalai Lama (1708–1757)

I bow at the feet of my guru, god of all gods.
O my kind teachers who revealed naked
the essence of mind primordially pure,
you are one with Manjushri and Tsongkhapa.

To a mind drunk with sleep, all dream objects,
the elephants and horses of illusion,
seem real; but in their place is nothing.
They are only creations of mind.

Likewise, self and others, bondage and release,
all phenomena are but constructs of words
and thinking; not an atom exists on its own,
save on the basis of designation and label.

Yet to the six senses of an ordinary being
veiled by the ignorance of deep sleep,
whatever appears seems objectively real.
We can see this by observing our unruly mind.

This objective reality of "self" and "the world"
created by our deluded mind is the object
to be negated in meditation's subtle probe;
destroy it, leaving no residue!

If "self" inheres in mind and body
over and above its mere name,

the self cannot depend on others:
"self" and *skandhas* are entirely separate—
like mountains in the eastern and western spheres.

Analyzed in terms of identity and difference,
examined by means of cause and effect,
not an atom exists in the "objective world."
The insight, which opens to the spacelike void,
which dawns through dismantling the solidity of things,
is the liberating vision, the view of emptiness.
Sustain mindfulness, affirm alertness,
attain thus the profound absorption—
the nonconceptual state of bliss
and clarity, apex of all meditations.

Immersed in this with one mind,
repeatedly probe the nature of things;
insight forceful as a thunderbolt—
indestructible weapon with a hundred spokes—
will arise to destroy the towering mountain
of grasping the real, of grasping the self.

In the aftermath of meditative equipoise
pure as the sky, the multitude of the codependent world
appears in perfect vividness like a rainbow;
all experiences and cognitions when unprobed
are mere deceptions, for nothing at all is real.

Joy and pain are like dreams;
material objects, a magician's show;
all sounds are echoes in empty caves.
Grasping them is children's play.

Yet, when a face and mirror
encounter each other, face-to-face,
there is an empty image.
There's no denying this!
Unfailing indeed is the power of dependence—
the union of appearance and voidness.
Engage with care in the discipline
of ethics, observe the difference of good and evil;
honor the precepts of all three vows.
With joyful mind seek the ultimate goal.

This body's a vessel filled with muck;
wealth is the bee's honey to be taken
by someone else; friends and family
are mere travelers gathered at a marketplace;
prosperity is but delusion's ploy, our enemy.

Life is a torrent raging down the stream,
so swiftly does it plunge toward its ruler, death.
Uncertain that we might still be alive at the day's end
when the sun reaches the mountains of the west,
we cling to the eight mundane concerns,
mere childish games, and scatter
to the wind our true concern—for freedom.
Unable at heart to see the fate
of beings so similar to oneself,
turn the mind to generate
the resolute wish for enlightenment.
Without this, even if you strive
with every fiber of body, speech, and mind,
in acts of virtue by both night and day
you can't approach the great way.

So rouse the perfect altruistic mind,
enter with force the bodhisattvas' way
by crossing the ocean of compassionate deeds,
taught in the sutra and tantra paths.

By the thunderous beat of the great summer drum
expounding view, meditation, and action,
may all beings awake from the slumber of ignorance
and achieve the bodhisattva's boundless aims.

Recognizing My Mother

Changkya Rölpai Dorje (1717–1786)

Emaho!

You who reveal the naked
wonders of profound dependent nature,
O guru, your kindness is boundless.
Kindly reside in my heart,
as I utter three spontaneous lines
from the thoughts flashing through my mind.

This lunatic child
who lost his mother long ago
will soon learn by pure chance
that he just failed to recognize her.
She was with him all along!

Perhaps mother is the yes and no of emptiness,
as whispered to me by my father,
dependent origination. All duality is
mother's benign smile; the cycle
of life and death, her verbal display.

Always truthful mother, you have fooled me!
I now seek salvation through my father's lore.
Yet, ultimately it is in you alone
that I can hope for freedom.

If the world is really what it seems to be,
even Buddhas of the three times cannot save me.

But this world of diversity and change
is actually my changeless mother's moods.
So I *can* hope for freedom!

Inexpressible mother unfixed
in any way or any place,
deceptively depending on things everywhere.
This dependence alone has deep meaning.

Not finding father, my cause, when sought,
is, in fact, the finding of mother;
and lo! father's found in mother's lap.
That is how the parents create us, I'm told!

It seems that my father's mirror
reflects nakedly my mother's face,
which is neither *one* nor *many*,
yet it's not obvious to a lunatic like me!

Based on the "instructions sent through the wind"
by masters Nagarjuna and Chandrakirti,
I am spared, by the light of insight,
the hardship of a long and arduous search.
So I hope to see my ever-present mother!

Among today's thinkers, there seem to be
some caught in the web of words:
"self-substantial," "ontologically real,"
and so on. They only invent monsters
with horns to negate, leaving intact
our vivid-gross-apparent world.

But in my mother's unveiled face
such vivid dualism's not found, I'm told!
Through proliferate discourses off the mark,
my mother is likely to run away!

Things exist, though not in this chaotic
concrete way that we perceive.
For the inseparable bond of our tender parents
appears in the form of harmony and love.

Vaibhashika, Sautrantika, Vijnanavada,
and the Eastern masters label the mother,
an elephant white as limestone,
with names so divergent and colorful:
"Atomic matter"—is she a beaming tiger?
"Intrinsic subject"—is she a crazy monkey?
"Absence of duality"—is she a wild bear?
They've all lost sight of dear, kind mother!

Likewise, many scholars and realized masters
of Sakya, Nyingma, Kagyü, and Drukpa
pride themselves in diverse terms:
"nonsubjective self-cognition of void and clear,"
"pristine purity and spontaneity, true face of
    Samantabhadra,"
"mahamudra, the innate uncontrived mind,"
"neither existent nor nonexistent, the viewless view."
It's all well if the target is hit;
but I wonder what they're aiming at!

The outer world is not dismantled,
O Vaibhashikas, be at ease.

Without self-cognition, perceptions arise,
O Vijnanavadins, be at ease.
Without intrinsic nature, dependence survives;
Eastern masters, be at ease.

As the void and the clear stand without contradiction,
Sakya upholders of pupil instructions,
you need not be alarmed.
Though pristinely pure, good and evil persist;
Nyingma knowledge bearers,
grasp not at purity.

Though imagined, the innate mind dawns;
Kagyü meditators, you need not protest.
Since the absence of dualism is fully accepted;
you hardened logicians need not fret.

Perhaps all this divergence evolved
due to unfamiliarity of standard conventions
by those who lack extensive learning.
It's not that I do not respect you;
please forgive me if I've offended.

Though I am not omniscient,
yet I possess the expertise
in skillfully riding the well-bred horse
of my forefathers' works.
Through an enduring, joyful exertion
I aspire to cross the impassable cliff.

No search is required, for the seeker is *it*;
never grasp *it* as real, for *it* is false;

yet this lie need not be resisted, for it *is* true.
Worthy indeed is this relaxation—
the freedom from two extremes.

Though lacking in coveted experience
of directly seeing the mother's face,
I feel as though I see in front of me
the kind parents so long lost!

Great indeed is the compassion
of Nagarjuna and his disciples;
great indeed is Lobsang Drakpa's kindness;
great indeed is my own guru's kindness.
In return, I venerate my mother.

By the joyous celebration of all good deeds,
through the meeting of my rikpa, the youthful son,
with my unborn, inexpressible mother,
may all beings be led to lasting bliss.

Ah! I, Rölpai Dorje,
perform here at this instant
a dance of ecstatic joy
to delight the Three Jewels.

*(These few deceptive lines describing the recognition of my mother
entitled "The Melodies of an Echo" were written by Changkya Rölpai
Dorje—someone with deep admiration for the great Middle Way—on
the mystical Mountain of Five Peaks.)*

Steps on the Path
to Awakening

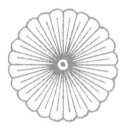

An Experiential Tune on Eight Dream Practices

Drakpa Gyaltsen (1147–1216)

I salute the assembly of gurus.

Towns, estates, and marketplaces
distract the untamed, wild-horse mind.
It's insight askew, like a broken peg,
the wild horse races amuck
unreined by the yoke of tranquil abiding.
As it gallops on the plain of bad action,
beware! It might fling you into the abyss!
So be a tame, or a wounded, beast,
live in the wild and meditate.

Disputes proliferate in company,
gossip arises in chat with a friend.
So, like an orphan, removed from the world,
live alone and meditate.

The fleeting praise of biased monks,
the respectful esteem of the monastery,
and the material offerings of lay devotees—
all three are the devil's flattery.
Practice dharma ceaselessly.

Too much attraction toward the surface,
too much attachment for wealth and possessions,
too strong a desire for food and drink—
these are disease for a meditator.

Cleanse the mind by the act of nongrasping;
practice dharma like an eager young boy.

Drinking alcohol, the destroyer of mindfulness,
eating meat, which undermines compassion,
womanizing, which corrodes one's fame—
these are ulcers in a meditator.
Pierce them with the firebrand of renunciation.
Practice dharma like a crazy person.

Keeping a vigil by a sick man's bed,
bringing up a child of a wealthy line,
making false clairvoyant claims—
these are wrong paths for a meditator.
Perceive offerings and service as evil.
Practice dharma like a stranger,
with no thought of reward.

The bliss of mental peace,
the unknowing that comes with that sensation,
meditations divorced from great compassion—
these are dangers for a meditator.
So, like great garuda cruising over the sky,
practice dharma by engaging in union.

Disciples filled with interest and respect,
family linked by karma,
fellow practitioners bound with pledges—
befriend them with an open heart.
But don't be distracted by fleeting affection.
Practice dharma: perceive all as dreams.

Lines of Self-Encouragement Written in Lhasa in the Year of the Horse

Rangjung Dorje, third Karmapa (1284–1339)

I prostrate to my gurus.

Without experience,
what others tell you is only words!
Without the guru's blessing,
though clever at words, you have no power.

Without faith rooted in the deeps,
clever words become mere ranting.
If existence is not rooted out,
even becoming a hermit is but form.

Without compassion rooted in the deeps,
working for others is but a pretense.
If volition is not rooted out,
knowing the causes is not a path.

Without seeing appearance as illusion,
closing the sense doors is still ignorance.
If nondual silence is not sought within,
insight is no more than verbal.

Without letting go of whatever occurs,
even "good" meditations are a samsaric route.
If every act is not sacredly purposeful,
your conduct ascends not above the world.

Without purifying the mental pollutants,
the so-called fruits aren't worth seeking.
If perceptions are not taken as metaphors,
the volumes of scriptures are but added words.

Without the essence of teachings deep in the heart,
all interpretations remain insignificant.
If empowerment does not touch the mind,
the multiple transmissions are but empty vases.

Without stable generation and its completion,
gathering disciples is nothing but form.
If tantric commitments are not fulfilled,
they bind like a leash pulling toward hell.

Without practicing what has been learned,
the wishes of the Buddhas are betrayed.
If you violate the sayings of the sages,
the seeds of *vajra* hell are sown.

If you cling to the practices of meditation,
you internally cling to destructive views.
If you are caught in any form of grasping,
you are ensnared in the *maras'* long noose.

I, Rangjung Dorje, wrote these lines,
aiming to stir myself; abandoning
everything hindering the practice,
I hold fast in factors of dharma.

I train myself to be free of clinging,
in conducive and adverse conditions.
I have written this piece out of my experience
in Lhasa in the year of the horse.

Wielding a Club in the Darkness

Tsangpa Gyare (1161–1211)

I salute the Precious One.

O Jhangchup Shönu, important man.
Oh dear, how very sad!
You do not see as dharma,
the acts of the guru, unsurpassed—
trunk of the mantra tree, the tantra tree!
Oh, listen to this tune.

Even when he is acting as a guru,
you do not see his work as dharma,
you're under the spell of apathy;
Fearful is the demon of spiritual sloth!
Follow the example of supreme Milarepa.

If, when engaged in hard dharma practice,
you bear not the trials of pleasure and pain,
you're under the spell of gratification.
Fearful is the demon of instant joy!
Follow the example of great Marpa Lotsawa.

If, when supplicating supreme gurus,
you cannot bear harsh words or beating,
you're under the spell of perverted views.
Fearful is the demon of negative thinking.
Follow the example of Pandit Naropa.

If entangled in the lure of food and clothes,
your mind wanders to the town of hungry ghosts,
you're under the spell of ghostly demons.
Fearful is the demon of wandering ghosts.
Follow the example of Buddha Shakyamuni.

When entranced by the pleasures of a prosperous town,
you're under the spell of indifferent apathy;
Fearful is the demon of spiritual poverty.
Follow the example of faithful Ananda.

If, within the ever-present sphere of nondoing,
mundane chores arise in the mind,
you're under the spell of desire and aversion.
Fearful is this demon of longing and hate.
Follow the example of Bengung Gyalpo.

If, working for the welfare of other beings,
you feel saddened by the treacherous and the hostile,
you're under the spell of self-absorption.
Fearful is the demon of calm and peace!
Follow the example of King Chandraprabha.

Instructions are like wielding a club in the darkness:
when given to one man, they succor another;
when given to all, someone is hurt.
Like the wealth of a rich man, they are transient.
Note with care the meaning of these words.

A Song of Self-Encouragement toward True Renunciation

Chone Lama Rinpoche (b. 1816)

O guru Vajradhara, all refuges embodied,
my father Khenchen Ngagi Wangpo,
sustain me with loving-kindness,
immerse my heart in the dharma.

My mind is long ingrained
in nondharma—since beginningless time—
not once does it immerse itself
in the virtuous, white karma;
I have wasted my entire life.

Quite apart from the stores of evil karma
piled from past lives, even in this life alone
I've heaped evil as high as a mountain;
nothing good can be said of my desperate fate.

One thing is sure to come, yet cannot be predicted:
what shall I do if I'm caught suddenly
unawares by Yama, lord of death?
What guarantee that I'll not descend into the worlds of hell?

If I do fall into this abyss,
even if I cry aloud and plead,
while in the unbearable, agonizing pains,
who will be my refuge then?

If you care for your own well-being,
leave aside mundane concerns;
practice dharma—which alone helps
when death's terrifying messenger comes.

"Fame is the devil's handheld fan;
wealth is a poison-coated sweet;
friends and relatives, mere passersby."
Reflect on these the words of the wise.

When speaking of samsara's pain
and especially of the lower realms,
the wise man's voice softens,
tears fall from his eyes,
his heart is stirred by empathy.

The great Marpa of Lhodrak said:
"If we are to describe in depth
all the sufferings of samsara,
we will never finish, even with a hundred tongues
and speaking all the time."

Cross to the shore of the jewel land
of permanent joy, if you are wise.
Build the boat of the three disciplines—
the sole raft to sail the ocean of samsara.

By virtue of reciting these lines to myself,
may I find without hardship
the precious mind of renunciation,
and embark on the path of the three disciplines.

Laying the Ground for Forbearance

Rangjung Dorje, third Karmapa (1284–1339)

I prostrate to my gurus.

Oh, you who are immersed in meditative practice
and have vestiges of virtuous karma,
this is the essence of spiritual practice:
the multitude of dualistic efforts
are but the means to realize
the nondual inner radiance.

If the beginner's stage brings
firmness but not clarity,
view the perceptions of the five sense doors
as unobstructed true essence.

If the beginner's stage brings
clarity but not great bliss,
know that perception of mind and object
is but a creative play of bliss.

If the beginner's stage brings
bliss but not the void,
seal the nature of four joys
with the unborn, emptiness.

Even those yogins who possess these three,
without the reins of mindfulness,

cannot quell conditioning's force.
Sustain mindfulness, distraction-free.

Even those yogins who possess these four,
without meditation's perfected skill,
cannot open the clairvoyant and supernatural door.
Train in the art of deep seeing.

Though clairvoyance and supernatural feats be achieved,
if compassion's perfect skill is not applied,
true altruistic action cannot be attained.
Strive in the four precepts benefiting others.

The result of all this endeavor:
all apprehensions of being are purged,
both for samsara and nirvana,
and all things dependently originated.
This is what the bodhisattvas perceived.
Thus realizing the voidness is bearable.
Affirming all things with the seal of emptiness
is called mahamudra, the great seal.
Fully realizing this truth,
work for others till the end of time.

On How to Engage in a Meditative Path

Drakpa Gyaltsen (1147–1216)

My clear-headed son, blessed with leisure,
faithful in fearing death and rebirth,
obedient in the conduct of your life,
my meditating son, keep this in your heart:

For deep meditation, you need firm resolve,
rooted in the bone of your heart,
renunciation, the core of mountain solitude.
Give up the concerns of everyday life.

For the growth of insight, you need pure pursuit
of the precepts and the three vows,
the ebbing of conceit and self-regard.
Take upon your crown care for all beings.

To receive the blessings of the masters,
honor them as enlightened Buddhas
and follow their example in your practice.
Evoke without ceasing their inspiration.

Let not views lead you astray;
perceive all phenomena as mind.
Purify into the essence every no and every yes,
samsara and nirvana, even he who says yes and no.

In meditation, be free of all apprehension,
in radiant experience, be free of all grasping,

find a haven, though the ground is lost.
Tread beyond every word, every thought.

Don't discard in your conduct judgments of no and yes,
but be free from thoughts of duality.
Trample upon the eight worldly concerns.
Be free of the antidotes, those "good" concepts too.

Aspire not to future results—
let realizations be manifest in you,
merge equipoise and aftersessions,
and eradicate all desire of endeavor.

To work for the welfare of sentient beings,
your prayer's propulsion must reach its peak
in the auspicious conjunction of cause and conditions.
Enhance nonobjectifying compassion.

This faint tune of eight pleas
is sung for those with clear perceptions.
Make your life great in realization.
And until then, cultivate resilience in meditation.

A Prayer for the Flourishing of Virtues

Tsongkhapa (1357–1419)

I prostrate to the Buddhas and their children throughout the
ten directions.

To free countless beings from samsaric existence,
with a pure heart I make this infinite prayer;
by the force of the infallible Three Jewels
and the powers of the great sages,
may these words of truth become real.

May I never be born again
in states where I descend to the lower realms;
may I attain the perfect human form
with spiritual freedom and opportunity.

Right from birth, may I never be attached
to the pleasures of mundane joys;
and inspired by thoughts of renunciation,
may I strive without respite for the pure life.

May there be no obstacles to renunciation
from family, friends, or possessions;
and may I achieve without hardship
conditions favorable to monastic life.

After entering the order, may I never be stained
by transgressing any of the precepts—

whether natural or specially proscribed—
precepts taken before the ordained masters.

As a monk may I strive for aeons,
through myriad hardships, in all the profound
and vast practices of the great vehicle,
for the sake of all beings, who have been my mother.

The sublime teachers who possess
the unshakable courage to help others—their minds
replete with learning and experience, tranquil,
compassionate, disciplined—may they look after me.

As Sadaprarudita sought out and trusted Dharmodgata,
may I please my sublime spiritual master
undaunted by any cost to my body, life, or wealth,
and never for an instant displease him.

As Sadaprarudita was taught, may I too be instructed
in the meaning of transcendent wisdom—
profound, tranquil, and nondual—
untainted by misapprehension's muddy water.

May I never be swayed by evil friends
and teachers of nonvirtue who profess
views of permanence and nothingness—
outside the Buddha's profound intent.

May I free all beings from the ocean of samsara—
sailing the ship of learning, reflection, and meditation,
hoisting a powerful sail of pure, altruistic intention
propelled by the wind of unstinting vigor.

The more I study, and the more I give,
and the more my spirit is enhanced
by pure discipline and critical insight,
the more liberated may I be from thoughts of arrogance.

May I study to my heart's content
countless scriptures with the most learned masters,
whose discernment of the profound meanings
through flawless reasoning is unrivaled.

May I cut all threads of doubt
through contemplation on profound conclusions
by the application of the fourfold reasoning,
pursued day and night with vigor and diligence.

When I attain insight through reflection
on the ways of dharma extremely profound,
may I pursue the path by seeking solitude,
vigorously cutting all ties to this life.

When my heart bears the imprint of Buddha's teaching,
through learning, reflection, and meditation,
may thoughts cherishing my own happiness
and the thirst for existence vanish forever.

Destroying miserly thoughts through detachment
from all things that I possess,
may I give material help to others
and benefit them with the gift of dharma.

By observing until full enlightenment,
even the smallest precepts in the spirit of renunciation,

and not compromising them even at the cost of my life,
may I fly the victory banner of spiritual freedom.

When I see, hear, or have thought of
beings who insult me, beat me, or have hated me,
may I be free of anger and always express
their good qualities, practicing tolerance.

May I abandon the three types of laziness,
which obstruct the attainment of new virtues
and undermine those already attained.
May I thus develop perseverance.

Discarding mere tranquil abiding of mind,
the ground for samsaric rebirth—
which lacks the insight outshining existence
and the moist compassion surpassing peace—
may I practice the union of calm abiding and insight.

By discarding all false views that hold supreme
views of emptiness speculative or incomplete,
upheld through fear of the profound mode of being,
may I realize all things as primordially void.

May I lead to the pure discipline of dharma
even the degenerate who wear monk's robes,
whose precepts are stained by a soiled conscience
and who disregard deeds condemned by the noble ones.

May I also lead to the path praised by the sages
those discarding the right path by entering negative ones,

swayed by the urging of evil friends
and influenced by teachers of nonvirtue.

The lion's roar of teaching, debate, and writing
humbles those false teachers, the foxes;
by caring for them through skillful means,
may I raise the banner of everlasting dharma.

When I drink the nectar of Buddha's words,
may I enjoy good birth, appearance, and wealth,
be skilled, intelligent, and live long,
wherever I may be reborn.

May I love more dearly even than my mother
those who have harmful intentions
toward my body, life, and possessions,
and those who speak evil against me.

By generating swiftly in their hearts
the bodhi mind that holds others dearer than self—
this pure, wondrous motivation—
may I lead them to unsurpassed enlightenment.

Whoever sees or hears
or contemplates these prayers,
may they never be discouraged
in seeking the boddhisattva's amazing aspirations.

By praying with such expansive thought
created from the power of pure intention,
may I achieve the perfection of prayers
and fulfill the wishes of all sentient beings.

Visions of
Mystic Consciousness

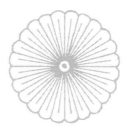

A Taste of Meditation

Tsangpa Gyare (1161–1211)

I salute the Precious One.

In the celestial palace of my guru's body
reside my parents—emptiness and compassion.
Don't cling to your mortal parents;
I'll give you father and mother eternal!

In the celestial palace of self-renunciation
is the wish-granting jewel of generosity.
Break the chains of miserliness;
I'll give you inexhaustible wealth!

In the celestial palace of uncharted wilderness
is the immutable haven of ever-presence.
Don't cling to objects of habit;
I'll give you an eternal home!

In the celestial palace of nondual bliss
is the stainless food of wisdom.
Don't be attached to tastes of the tongue;
I'll give you the taste of meditation!

In the celestial palace of appearance and emptiness
is the Buddha's body of transcendent illusion.
Identify not with your physical form;
I'll give you an indestructible form!

In the celestial palace of the heart, the sacred image
accomplishes the interest of self and others.
Be driven not by the devil of discrimination;
I'll give you emptiness and compassion!

In the nondual samsara-nirvana palace
resides the king free of hope and apprehension.
Be not oppressed by the weight of eight concerns;
I'll lead you to the city of the three kayas!

The Dakinis' Feast

Natsok Rangdröl* (b. 1608)

I salute my father gurus.
Of unmistaken lineage from Naropa,
I sing this song of joy with joyfulness.
Listen, you, assembled at the feast.

The unchanging sky of day
and the Milky Way that suddenly appears at night
seem distinct to our fleeting, false perception.
Yet within the space of essence, they merge into one.

The waters of the never-ending Tsangpo River
and the streams that spill from the monsoon rains
are separated by gorges, countries, the terrain.
Yet within the great ocean they merge into one.

The great inspiration of my father gurus,
the force of my love and respect for them,
seem to be separate, in different bodies.
Yet within the mind of essence, they merge into one.

I offer this feast to you, O the Three Jewels.
Be immersed in this musical feast, O dakinis.
Auspicious indeed is to be free of hindrance.
Prosperity will shower upon you, assembled at the feast.

* Although our source literature lists the author as Natsok Rangdröl, this poem may
actually have been written by Milarepa.—EDS.

An Adamantine Song on Purposeless Pursuits

Longchen Rabjampa (1308–1363)

My precious guru, I beseech you;
attend me with compassion, bless me.
In this life, the next, and in between, at all times,
be my refuge and my protector, be my friend.

Too entrenched in the delusions of self-grasping,
I haven't reached the ground of essence, the enlightened intent.
If the lasting haven, the cognition of being, is not attained,
what use have I of land, house, or family?

Too attached to the deluded friendship of afflictions—
the spontaneous, inner radiance remains far away.
If I do not make friends with this inseparable companion,
what use have I for illusory life partners?

Burdened by the guardianship of children and grandchildren—
the natural glow of self-arisen rikpa is lost.
If the youth of the mind's inner radiance is absent,
what use have I of children born of fate?

Too devoted to the circle of family and friends,
wish granting and supportive—my inborn
self-reliance on wisdom is abandoned.
And then, what use are friends, family, and supporters?

Too reliant on the security of wealth and possession—
the joy of rikpa, primordial and accomplished,

is lost. Devoid of the resources of meditative attainment,
what use have I for the material resources of this life?

Clinging to the riches of an illusory world,
I lose the wish-granting jewel; the inner radiance
of mind stripped of the noble gem of contentment,
what use have I for worldly belongings?

Too occupied by pretension, fame, and appearance—
what time is there to accomplish meditation?
If I do not practice dharma from the heart with effort,
what gain is there even if I appear prosperous?

Days and nights spent in acts of distraction—
what chance is there to attain the experience of being?
If I fail to follow in the footsteps of past masters,
what use have I for sense-enhancing diversions?

Too attached to the savor of fame, esteem, and service,
there seems little freedom from the eight worldly concerns.
If clinging and craving are not cleansed like the sky,
what benefit even if I appear wise?

By tinkering with my self-image for worldly effect,
how can I secure the undeceiving, my own true face?
If the senselessness is not appreciated from the heart,
what value is there in seeming impressive?

Pursuing too much "others' interest" after losing one's own,
what leisure or freedom to practice the dharma?
If I don't give up devotion to obstructive dependents,
what use am I, though seeming greatly altruistic?

Giving too much time to insignificant affairs,
there is no space to attain the wisdom of nonduality.
If I do not demolish the habit of appeasement,
what use have I for expectations of gratitude?

Being occupied with mundane things, day and night,
what time have I to attain the nondoing essence?
If I do not discard at once these deluded engagements,
what use do I have for meaningless pursuits?

Depending too much on groups and society,
I lose the chance to practice dharma in solitude.
If I do not seek solitude and the wilderness,
what use have I for places of distraction?

Too engaged in virtuous deeds tainted by distractions,
today there is no chance even to secure the foundations
of the path. If I do not discard worldly norms
from the heart, what use is the appearance of virtue?

When one is too attached to objectifying views,
there seems no space to cross the sky of essential rikpa.
If I fail to purge the contrived appearances of subject and object,
what use are the slight signs of heat generation?

Reliant too much on the mentality of gradual effort,
how can I realize the true intent, beyond cognition?
If I do not meditate on the Great Perfection heart drops,
what use have I of dharmas that grasp at the extremes?

O you who aspire for liberation,
enter the unsurpassed, the great secret;

alone in the wilderness, put your heart in meditation.
In this life, you can secure the eternal dharmakaya.

This song was sung by Longchen Rabjampa Zangpo,
a yogin of the king among vehicles;
by the merits of this song, may all beings without limit
be totally free and become the ever-perfect Kuntu Zangpo.

(Longchen Rabjampa, the yogin of the Great Natural Perfection, wrote the above poem at the hermitage of Lhundrup Ling.)

A Dance of Unwavering Devotion

Chone Lama Rinpoche (b. 1816)

You who absorb into sublime, immutable bliss
all phenomena, moving and unmoving, infinite as space,
O glorious Heruka and Varahi, your consort,
I wear the jewel light of your feet as my crown.

Great bliss, the union of method and wisdom,
engaged in the play of the unmoving with movement,
this young coral maiden with beautiful eyes,
diamond queen, embrace me with your arts of love.

Adorning the highest part of my body,
my crown, with the jewel of your feet,
I recite these words of aspiration and prayer
with my palms folded at my heart.

When shall I ever achieve this state:
seeing all forms as mandala deities,
all sounds as vajra songs of tantra,
all thoughts as fuel to enflame
the spontaneous wisdom of emptiness and bliss?

When will I experience perfect purity?
By purging in profound absorption
all phenomena born of imaginative concepts,
fully aware that they open the way to self-arisen rikpa.

When will I run in a joyful step-dance,
the play of supreme illusion, the bliss-void wisdom,

in the dakini town, the emanation of pure realms—
where a hundred dharma doors are opened wide?

Outer dakinis hover above the twenty-four mystic places;
inner dakinis dwell in the sphere of radiant bliss.
When will I immerse in the glory of sexual play
through the secret act of conjoining space and vajra?

When can I arise as the great magical net—
the union of body and mind,
instantly burning all grossness of dualism
with the great bliss fire flaming the expanse?

When will I accomplish the natural feat
of absorbing the imperfections of illusion
into immutable bliss, this wheel of becoming,
engaged in the blissful play of union?

On the clear mirror of the luminous mind
my guru, my deity, and my mind reflect as one;
may I soon attain the good fortune of
practicing night and day this perfect meditation.

May my mind be always intoxicated
by drinking insatiably the nectar—
the delicious taste of sexual play
between the hero in his utter ecstasy
and his lover, the lady emptiness.

By entering deep into the sphere of voidness,
may I be endowed with the power of cleansing

this foul odor, grasping body, speech, and mind as ordinary,
through the yoga perceiving all as divine.

May I come to see with naked eyes
the form of the fully emergent mandala
of perfect deities, the sport of the ever-present mind
inside the courtyard of the heart's dharma chakra.

O yoginis, heroines of the twenty-four places,
and the hosts of mantra-born and field-born dakinis
who possess powers swift as thought,
assist me in friendship of every kind.

A Song on the View of Voidness

Karma Trinley (1456–1539)

Homage to the Adamantine Mind!

Dharma king, you who have realized
the essence; you who expound
the way of being, out of compassion:
kind Buddha Samdrup,
I bow to you in my heart,
pray listen to me.

Through your kind and skillful means,
by a habit long formed, and as a fruit
of long practice in this life,
I have realized the nature of ever-presence.

When the secret of appearance is revealed,
everything arises in a tone of voidness,
undefined by the marks of identity.
Like a sky that is nothing but an image.

When the secret of thoughts is revealed,
though active, they are but mind's sport,
naked reflections of transcendent mind
unsullied by deliberation and correction.

When the secret of recollection is revealed,
every memory is but an illumination

of self-knowledge in the ever-present state,
untainted by ego consciousness.

When the secret of illusions is revealed,
they seem nothing but the primordial state,
appearing in the visual field of rikpa,
untouched by the dualism of mind and things.

When the secret of abiding is revealed,
you are in the state of self-cognition,
however long you remain, free of elaboration,
the expanse unstained by laxity and torpor.

When the secret of mobility is revealed,
however much you move, you remain
within clear light, unstained by distraction,
excitement, and so on, a true self-recognition.

When the secret of samsara is revealed,
however often one may circle, the cycles
are illusion unaffected by joy and pain.
This is the realization of Buddha's four bodies.

When the secret of peace is revealed,
however tranquil one's attainments,
they are but an image; this is the natural pure space,
free of the signs of being and nonbeing.

When the secret of birth is revealed,
however one's reborn, it's but an emanation;
meditation's vision of pure self-generation
free of clinging and apprehensions.

When the secret of death is revealed,
however often one may die, it's but the vision
of the ultimate, the stages of completion
perfect, free of any karmic deeds.

When the secret of bliss is revealed,
its intensity cannot be bettered;
this is the state of spontaneous bliss,
free of all traces of contamination.

When the secret of luminosity is revealed,
however bright, it's but an empty form—
mother image of the void in space,
free of every multiplicity.

When the secret of emptiness is revealed,
though empty, it is the unsurpassed,
devoid of every contingent stain,
and free from every deception.

When the secret of the view is revealed,
however much one looks and sees,
the world remains beyond thought and word—
the expanse beyond dichotomies.

When the secret of meditation is revealed,
however much one meditates, it's but a state—
undistracted, and in natural restfulness,
free of exertion and constraint.

When the secret of action is revealed,
whatever one does are the six perfections—

spontaneous, free, and to the point,
uncolored by strictures and moral codes.

When the secret of fruition is revealed,
achievements are but the cognition
of mind as dharmakaya,
the mind itself free of hope and fear.

This is the profound innermost secret;
guru's blessings have entered my heart;
naked nonduality dawns within;
the secret of samsara and nirvana is revealed!

I have beheld the face of the ordinary mind;
I have arrived at the view that is free of extremes;
even if the Buddha came in person now,
I have no queries that require his advice!

This song on the view of voidness
expounding the nature of the being of all,
spoken in words inspired by conviction,
was sung in a voice echoing itself,
unobstructed, in between meditation sessions.

On How to Apply the Antidotes

Drakpa Gyaltsen (1147–1216)

To a mind unsettled in itself,
no pursuit can offer peace;
if all things are not perceived as mind,
delusions of variety arise.
I have ceased to believe in appearances now.
Why should I, a beggar, make much of such things now!
All paths to enlightenment,
both equipoise and aftersession states,
arise within the vastness of the Great Seal.

When food is not perceived as sacred nectar,
preferences of better and worse arise.
I have ceased to believe in such nourishment as real.
Why should I, a beggar, search for such food now!
The food that enters the mouth sustains the body.
All this is in the vastness of the Great Seal.

When all appearances are not perceived as scripture,
there is no end to proliferating words.
I have ceased to believe in the words and letters of scripture.
Why should I, a beggar, bother with the texts now!

To one receptive, even a word of dharma is precious.
When the dharma is not perceived in terms of the Great Seal—
that the mind is the master of samsara and nirvana—
clinging to my circle of disciples arises.

I have ceased to trust those attached to others.
Why tame now the untamed beggar's mind!

The six mindfulnesses are friends of enlightenment;
all lies within the vastness of the Great Seal;
I sang this song in a state of melancholy;
I have sung it by applying the antidotes of mind.

Cutting the Rope of Conceit

Machik Labdrön (1055–1143)

The fruition of the three kayas unfolds
from body, speech, and mind;
Buddhahood cannot be attained elsewhere.
If this goal is sought outside oneself,
even the efforts of countless aeons
will fail to bear any fruit.
Search not, strive not;
let your mind rest in its natural state.
Supreme "cutting off" of the ego
is the liberating absence of effort—
free of all limitations of hope and fear.
When you cut the rope of grasping,
where can there be Buddhahood?

Although the scriptures speak of four demons,
all are subsumed within conceit.
Grasping at appearances as if they were real,
that is the demon that obstructs wisdom.
All attachment and repulsion to things of the world
have their roots in conceit.
You're freed of grasping when conceit's rope is cut.
As by killing the fire itself,
even smoke in wall crevices is quenched.
The objects do not cease,
though they have been negated.
By seeing the absence of ground,
the demons are finally defeated.

For a skilled magician,
perception does not lead to clinging.
Therefore cut the rope of conceit.
The act of cutting does not destroy it,
but the awareness of groundlessness
leaves no room for grasping.
You're freed in the expanse of reality's essence.
All demons are destroyed in conceit-free states.
I, Labdrön, who am carefree, treasure this.

A Feast Song in Lhasa

Rangjung Dorje, third Karmapa (1284–1339)

I salute the guru jewel.

In the ocean of true essence
arise multitudes of unreal concepts,
like varied patterns in the water.
Therefore I practice the following.

This heroic feast—the culmination of merit
for the profound mother tantra—
was taught to increase the merit of beings.
Thus do I understand its meaning:

Beings of the beginning stage
should visualize their body as a deity
at this stage of imaginative engagement.
Purify food and drink into nectar,
and offer the skandhas to the victorious sages.
This is called the great feast:
heroes and heroines equal in number,
who have attained high realizations,
contemplate the essence of void and bliss
amid an abundance of food and drink.
Great is the assembly at the feast!
Since all heroes have gathered,
it is called the joyous feast of heroes.
The master knows the way of mantra,
his mindstream is empowered,

he understands the essential precepts;
disciple-hosts of heroines and heroes,
together engage in full absorption—
the stages of generation and its completion—
immeasurable are the attainments of the feast.
Those who do not possess such virtues,
and wrongly partake out of self-importance,
will encounter obstacles; this is foretold.
Though I have not seen the assembled heroes,
I have sung the essence of the tantric scriptures;
for this is called the essential instruction.
Be inspired with wondrous admiration.
Join the celebration, partake fully in the feast!

(This poem was sung in Lhasa at the assembly gathered to celebrate a religious feast on the evening of the eighth day of the tenth month of the dragon year.)

Hail to Manjushri!

Rangjung Dorje, third Karmapa (1284–1339)

All phenomena are like illusions,
though absent they appear to exist;
wise indeed are those who cognize them
within the ever-present unborn.

If you perceive the glorious guru
as a supremely enlightened being
indivisible from your own mind,
you will receive blessings and strength.

If you, without ceasing, propel the flow
of channels, wind energies, and vital drops—
the nexus of interdependent factors—
the stains of self-love will be swiftly cleansed.

The manifold states of nonconception—
clarity and bliss—I place on the path
of nonapprehension, like patterns in water,
then the true mode of being will be definitely seen.

A Vajra Song Aspiring to Tread the Footsteps of the Heroes

Chone Lama Rinpoche (b. 1816)

Though eternally asleep in the expanse of nondual bliss,
radiating playful emanations covering all space,
O guru Heruka, mandala heroes and heroines,
dance in the heart chakra, the seat of the five vital drops.

I am saddened by the life of endless suffering,
caught by childish toys of mundane pleasures;
today I sing a song as words come freely to my mouth,
resounding the tune of thought's spontaneous flow.

The arrows of woman's sensual beauty
constantly pierce my youthful heart—
as I cling to the view that forms are real,
the swinging from joy to pain never seems
to cease; this is karma's force.

How I wish to look to my heart's content
at the smiling face of the great bliss queen:
the dawning of the view that no objects are real,
by seeing through the illusion of a solid world.
May I rest at will in the space free of clinging.

The showering darts of women's seductive smiles,
the vanity that sees praise and blame as real,
these are empty echoes—mere phantoms on a mirror's
    face—

yet they hit and hurt the target of my heart
and lead to pain, to illness so hard to escape.
Is there no cure from this habit long formed?

How I wish to hear the sweet tunes in my ears,
the unceasing vajra mantra of the breath's natural tone,
engendered by winds that carry ever-present bliss.
May I perfect the view that hears all sounds as empty echoes.

Form is empty: yet the seductress who deludes me
that forms are real repeatedly tears at my lustful heart.
Terrible it is, that there's no release from this pain,
duhkha eating at the root of all goodness.

By cutting off this fantasy, bad fortune's solicitation,
the hero of great bliss who sees everything as empty
embraces the heroine, self-expression of nondual space and
    awareness.
How I wish to experience the bliss of union!

May I generate true feelings of revulsion
for the duhkha nature of samsaric joys.
May I travel to the security of blissful freedom.
How I wish to liberate beings infinite as space!

HA, HA, the supreme, noble fruits of such prayers,
HEH, HEH, may we have the fortune to know them.
KYE, HO, you who take pride in youth and intoxicants,
AH, HO, you've lost the chance to taste bliss and joy.

Little Tiger

Kelsang Gyatso, seventh Dalai Lama (1708–1757)

The honey bee, a little tiger,
is not addicted to the taste of sugar;
his nature is to extract the juice
from the sweet lotus flower!

Dakinis, above, below, and on earth,
unimpeded by closeness and distance,
will surely extract the blissful essence
when the yogins bound by pledges gather.

The sun, the king of illumination,
is not inflated by self-importance;
by the karma of sentient beings,
it shines resplendent in the sky.

When the sun perfect in skill and wisdom
dawns in the sky of the illumined mind,
without conceit, you beautify
and crown the beings of all three realms.

The smiling faces of the radiant moon
are not addicted to hide and seek;
by its relations with the sun,
the moon takes waning and waxing forms.

Though my gurus, embodiment of all refuge,
are free of fluctuation and of faults,

through their flux-ridden karma the disciples perceive
that the [guru's] three secrets display all kinds of
    effulgence.

Constellations of stars adorning the sky
are not competing in a race of speed;
due to the force of energy's pull,
the twelve planets move clockwise with ease.

Guru, deity, and dakini—my refuge—
though not partial toward the faithful,
unfailingly you appear to guard
those with fortunate karma blessed.

The white clouds hovering above on high
are not so light that they arise from nowhere;
it is the meeting of moisture and heat
that makes the patches of mist in the sky.

Those striving for good karma
are not greedy in self-interest;
by the meeting of good conditions
they become unrivaled as they rise higher.

The clear expanse of an autumn sky
is not engaged in an act of cleansing;
yet being devoid of all obscuration,
its pure vision bejewels the eyes.

The groundless sphere of all phenomena
is not created fresh by a discursive mind;

yet when the face of ever-presence is known,
all concreteness spontaneously fades away.

Rainbows radiating colors freely
are not obsessed by attractive costumes;
by the force of dependent conditions,
they appear distinct and clearly.

This vivid appearance of the external world,
though not a self-projected image,
through the play of fluctuating thought and mind
appears as paintings of real things.

An Adamantine Song on the Ever-Present

Longchen Rabjampa (1308–1363)

To experience the ocean of essence,
resembling the sphere of unchanging space:
free of center and perimeter,
pervading the expanse.
Enlightened mind transcends cognition!

Rootless and baseless are appearance
and void, in the self-arisen rikpa
of every perception.
Vivid is the sense of noncessation:
luminous, the absence of object perception.

Within the voidness free of class distinction
all appearances dissolve, for their ground is lost;
The rikpa of liberation is spread evenly.
Subject and object are both void,
for their roots are lost.

The essence of self-arisen wisdom
and all duality are cleansed like the sky;
subjects and objects arise as free from bounds,
as naked dharmakaya!
This is the Great Perfection, free of cognition!

The self-arisen ground primordially pure,
the untraversed path supremely swift,
the unsought fruit spontaneously savored,

such is the Great Perfection,
in the radiant dharmakaya.

This primordial sphere of pervasive essence
is the Great Perfection of samsara
and nirvana; this song of transcending—
beyond cause and effect, beyond all endeavor,
was sung by Longchen Rabjam Zangpo.

*(This poem was written by Longchen Rabjampa, a yogin of the
supreme vehicle, at the hermitage of Lhundrup Ling.)*

On the Inner Practice of Secret Mantra

Drakpa Gyaltsen (1147–1216)

Supreme guru, great Vajradhara,
you who pacify beings of the three vehicles,
at your lotus feet I bow my head.

Sharpen the conduct of those under oath.
This is the essence and distillation
of the inner meaning of the secret mantra,
and the path of experiential practice.
Do not forget it, keep it fresh in the mind.

The guru is the root of powerful attainment.
Appease him with the three services.
Transgress not his advice
even if it cost you body and life.

Maintain a firm generation stage:
perceiving all beings, all environments,
as vivid manifestations of divine mandalas;
be utterly free of profane perceptions.

Apprehend the nature of nonduality,
rainbow fusion of appearance and emptiness,
engendered by the ending of "reality" grasping;
move toward the yoga of pure divine vision.

The interpenetration of wisdom and method,
the glow of unalloyed bliss,

the four joys—enlightened intention of the Buddhas.
Assimilate them so they merge into a single taste.

The sphere of E, perfect appearance and existence,
arises in diverse VAM guises.
Yet there is nothing that transcends E;
go beyond the mind to the union.

To overcome notions of cleanliness,
and attain the body of five lineages—
the pure state of five skandhas—
always be inseparable from the binding nectar.

The union of emptiness and compassion
is the essence of the great vehicle path.
Enhance the nonobjectifying bliss
without emitting veiled *bodhichitta*.

Bliss and emptiness are inseparable:
this is the essence of secret mantra.
Enhance the bliss of full detachment
without emitting *kunda*'s bodhichitta.

Dharmakaya is as pure as space:
this is the essence of the final tantra.
Seek the essence on all occasions
without emitting supreme bodhichitta.

Through three auspicious nonemissions,
control the apparent and the obscure.
Engaging in the four skillful actions,
liberate all spiritual aspirants.

May the mandala deities, peaceful and wrathful,
who have perfected merit and wisdom,
become fertile fields for realization.
May form and wisdom be harmonized.

At the Feet of the Lord of Dance

Karma Trinley (1456–1539)

I salute the Adamantine Mind.

I bow at the feet of the lord of dance,
my father, the glorious Chakrasamvara
in human form: true being of my savior,
the seminal HAM immersed
in great immutable bliss.

At dusk I endeavored in good deeds
and cleansed vices;
at night I immersed in the clear light of sleep;
at dawn I trained
in "blazing and melting," in "vital exertion";
I utter this song
as surges of bliss arise in me.

This is the cause that leads men to fight over rule and domain:
egoistic clinging increases attachment and enmity.
If such trivialities are discarded, we are joyful wherever we reside.
Happy is the wandering yogin without fixed abode.

Attachment to friends and family is the grip of samsara's chain;
distinctions between friend and foe thicken the five poisons of mind;
when the heart is pure, you can be friends with all;
happy is the yogin free of friend and enemy.

Worldly concerns are the leash of the demons;
deliberations of right and wrong increase attachment;

the way of dharma leads to spontaneous accomplishment;
happy is the yogin who has exorcised the demon of worldly greed.

The study of outer knowledge diverts from true learning and
    contemplation;
the scholars' debates based on reason and scripture proliferate
    concepts;
the supreme scholar is he who recognizes mind's own nature;
happy is the yogin who attains self-knowing awareness.

The dense line drawings of thought are samsara's origin;
grasping at the good and bad proliferates illusion;
perfect is the uncreated, the spontaneous; happy
the yogin who cultivates that beyond word and thought.

Perception of the ordinary is the clinging that binds us;
perception as pure divinity enhances wholesome consciousness;
happy, self-liberating, is the yogin who sees nakedly,
without any grasping, the union of emptiness and form.

The energies of karma and delusion are bondage's root;
when the great energy of concepts stirs, bondage is enforced.
Yet when the true face of this is perceived, it *is* the wisdom energy;
happy is the yogin who knows the great way of "vital exertion."

When the seminal essence degenerates, it leads to hell;
the bliss of melting divorced of attainment increases lust;
when it fills the site of great bliss—that is the path to awakening;
happy is the yogin expert in retention, inversion, and spreading.

One falls into self-absorption if led astray by emptiness divorced of
    form;

one multiplies samsara if attached to the forms of appearance;
happy is the yogin who abides in mahamudra, the spontaneous
    coalescence,
free from the qualities of the grasping and the grasped.

By the power of remembering my guru's kindness,
the experience of bliss arose within me,
and I sang this song early at dawn
between two sessions of meditation—
an adamantine poem of blissfulness.

In Response to a Request for Teaching on Cause and Effect

Drukpa Künlek (1455–1570)

The bed is the workshop of intercourse:
it is best when wide and soft.
Knees are the messengers of sex:
they should be set out in advance.
Arms are the straps of sex:
their grip must be a tight embrace.
Buttocks are the laborers of intercourse:
they must wheel around and around.
This is the discourse on what is possible.

Now, on what is not possible.
The clitoris is a luscious triangle;
it's not a *torma* to propitiate the spirits.
The anus may be full of long, strong hairs;
they cannot be used for sewing cloaks.
The scrotum may seem full and low;
it isn't a food bag for the hermit's fare.
Although the prick has a shaft and head;
it's not for hammering stakes into the ground.

Next follows the discourse on cause and effect.
If your words are hard, like a closed cunt,
no one will be your friend.
If your temperament is tender, like a vagina's lips,
everyone will be your friend.
Do not acquire the untamed character

of an untrimmed forest of pubic hair,
for if you do, you'll just offend.
He who is humble, like a flaccid penis
in its own warm juices, has many friends.
If you drift about like the smell of a fart,
no one will like you: you'll be shunned and lost.
Suppress bad speech, like a tight ass.
Ah, the clitoris rides astride,
the penis head has entered deep,
the scrotum sack is left outside,
with only the guard to keep!

The all-permeating view of nonduality
should have the female organ's depth and space.
The nongrasping meditation of clarity and emptiness
should be vibrant and clear as menstrual blood.
The merging of all tastes according to six cycles
should have the ecstasy of orgasmic meeting.
Endeavor in mantras and meditations
with the vigor of a donkey in copulation.
When engaging in these practices,
be spontaneous as a cock in penetration.
The strictures of a solitary retreat
should be tighter than a dog's copulation.

This discourse on mundane pleasures
will prick up the pangs of lust in the young.
Old ladies, remember your past of pleasures;
young tigers, put my injunction to the test!
The old have no regrets about matters of sex;
for virtuous celibates, it's an object of revulsion;
for the rich and powerful, sex is the truth;
for me, Drukpa Künlek, this is my practice.

Experience of the Single Taste

Za Paltrül Rinpoche (1808–1887)

When your grasping mind engages
an object real but illusory,
the illusion may deceive the mind.
Yet object and mind—like the moon and its reflection—
are of a single taste, though they seem to be two.
That is, if you truly know it.

When an old man's eye wanders
toward a body of youthful flesh,
it may bring to life the corpse of his lust.
If body attachment is freed within the expanse,
youth and old age become a single taste.

When you perceive the three stages
of birth and rebirth as permanent,
the pain of death may indeed be intense.
Yet in the essence of pristine consciousness,
birth and death are of a single taste.

When the strings of love are tight
for family and friends,
the stress of separation may be intense.
Yet, if you know the nature of samsara,
coming together and parting are of a single taste.

When you expect too much from the gods,
you may suspect a devil's work.
Yet if you see the whole world as a god,
god and devil become a single taste.

When you pursue the trail of thoughts too far,
hundreds of things you need to do come to mind.
Yet when you glimpse the nonconceptual mind,
you can sleep like a carcass, free of deeds.

If you listen to everything people say,
you freeze—for there is nothing you can do.
Yet when you determine your own fate,
you can instantly turn the mind inward.

Your qualities are greater when others see them.
Yet when you know your own faults,
there is no room for self-delusion.
It is time to bury the evil corpse.

Reflections on the
Poet's Own Life

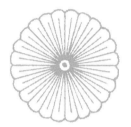

Old Dog in the Wilderness

Za Paltrül Rinpoche (1808–1887)

I prostrate at the feet of the guru.

As this old dog was living in the wilderness,
it heard the voice of its sublime refuge, guru,
and felt compelled to utter the following lines:

When I first met my guru,
I was filled with expectations,
like a sailor on the shores of a land of gold!
That is how I began my spiritual quest.

When in midlife I met my guru,
I was assailed with guilt,
like a convict face-to-face with an official.
The guru's discipline was harsh.

When I see my guru now,
I have a sense of brotherhood,
like pigeons sleeping together in a temple roof.
So I live afar from the guru now.

When I first received the pith instructions,
I had the urge to gulp it all at once,
like a starving man face-to-face with food.
That was the way I engaged in practice!

When in midlife I received the instructions,
I was plagued with wavering doubts,

as if hearing faint echoes of a distant sound.
The threads of my apprehensions remained uncut.

When I hear the instructions now,
I feel a sense of revulsion,
like a man made to eat his own vomit.
The desire to listen no longer exists.

When I first sought solitude,
I felt a sense of total ease,
like a traveler just returning home.
I was happy in the wilderness.

When in midlife I sought solitude,
I felt a sense of restlessness,
like a beautiful woman on her own.
I was constantly on the move.

When I seek solitude now,
I feel that I am on secure ground,
like an old dog lying dead under a crevice.
Have I finally hidden my corpse?

When I first contemplated the view,
the higher I soared, the more excited I felt,
like a vulture searching for a nesting place.
But my view was confined to words.

When in midlife I reflected on the view,
I had fears of going astray,
as if negotiating a treacherous pass.
I stayed mainly in silence.

When I contemplate the view now,
I feel as if deceived,
like the way grown-ups fool children.
I find nothing in which to trust my mind.

When I first began meditating,
I felt a surge of bliss,
like a couple in love gazing on each other.
I was eager to undertake meditation.

When in midlife I meditated,
I felt a sense of tiredness and exhaustion,
like a weakling weighed down by a load.
My sessions were indeed short!

When I think of meditation now,
I cannot bear an additional instant,
feeling that I carry the universe on a stone slab.
I have no desire to practice further.

When I think of my conduct as I began,
I felt rigidly tied by the precepts,
like a wild horse tamed for the first time.
My behavior had a false discipline.

When I think of my conduct in midlife,
I felt a sense of total abandon,
like a dog pulled loose from its chain.
I lost the grip of moral rules.

When I reflect on my conduct now,
I have a sense of familiarity,

like a whore who leaves her trade out of boredom.
I sense an apathy toward joy and pain.

When I first thought about results,
I had expectations of great achievement,
like a devious trader who barters for gain.
Those were my hopes and my greed.

When in midlife I thought of results,
I sensed an unreachable goal,
like being separated on two sides of an ocean.
Discouraged was my state of mind.

When I think about results now,
I feel a lack of resourcefulness,
like a thief whose last refuge is darkness.
Such is the level of my despair.

When I first began to teach,
I felt the urge to display my wisdom,
like a beauty who finds herself in a crowd.
Such was my appetite for speaking.

When in midlife I taught the dharma,
a sense of familiarity arose with the theme,
like an old man telling old stories.
The profusion of speech was indeed too much.

When I teach today,
I feel the urge to reveal my faults,
as if entranced by the spell of a spirit.
Such is my sense of embarrassment.

When I first entered disputation,
I felt the urge to win in debate,
like a skillful lawyer at work.
Such was the extent of my hostility.

When in midlife I engaged in debate,
I felt a yearning for truth,
like an unbiased jury seeking a verdict.
I was committed then to the task.

When I engage in debate now,
I feel I could say anything,
like a cheat who wanders from place to place.
Thus far have I roamed from propriety.

When I first began writing,
I felt a surge of inspiration,
like the *mahasiddhas* uttering their songs.
My style was natural then.

When I wrote in midlife,
I felt compelled to attend to the words,
like a skilled poet writing his verses.
I was dedicated to composition.

When I sit to write now,
I feel it's all meaningless,
like writing guidebooks without the experience.
I no longer waste the paper and ink.

When I first began making friends,
I had a strong sense of competition,

as if powerful tigers were on parade.
High were the levels of pride and envy.

As I related to friends in midlife,
I felt I had to please them all,
like a prostitute in the marketplace.
That is why I had so many "friends."

When I relate to friends now,
I feel I don't belong in the group,
like an awkward adolescent in a crowd.
Like a loner, I stay alone.

When I first tasted wealth and possessions,
I felt an instant gratification,
like children gathering flowers.
I never hoarded or tried to collect.

When in midlife I thought of wealth,
I felt an insatiable greed,
like trying to fill a pot with a hole at the base.
This is why my finds were so few.

When I see wealth and possessions now,
I feel the weight of their burden,
like an old man with too many kids.
Joyful am I, in poverty.

When I first attracted attendants and servants,
I felt I was taking care of them,
treating them as paid workers.
False was the altruism of such deeds.

When in midlife I had such dependents,
I felt my freedom violated,
like a novice who resents his guardian.
So I cut the threads of association.

When I interact with servants now,
I feel everything is misplaced or broken,
as if a dog has been let loose in the house.
I walk alone now without any aid.

When I first attracted disciples,
I was filled with self-importance,
like an official with many deputies.
I indulged in self-congratulation.

When in midlife I had disciples,
I felt the need to rely on them,
like guests arriving from holy places.
Such was the extent of my urge to help.

When disciples come to me now,
I feel a sense of annoyance,
like stirring up spirits in haunted places.
I chase them away with stones in my hand.

A Song of Repentance and Disclosure

Tsangpa Gyare (1161–1211)

I salute the Precious One.

O Vajradhara, the chief of all saviors—
the refuge of all, protector of beings—
without moving from your unborn sphere,
As in a dream, hear my confession.

O perfect gurus and mandala deities,
whose emanation is Vajradhara,
I've fallen beneath heedless delusion,
I repent and purge my views and deeds.

O the Three Jewels, refuge of sentient beings,
I repent and disclose to you
my transgression of your instructions:
not seeking for liberation,
the supreme medicinal cure.

O all-accomplishing mandala deities
responsive to the inclinations of all,
I repent the shortcomings in my meditation:
I've followed the habits of flesh and blood.

O powerful protectors and dakinis,
the spirits defending the doctrine,
I repent my faults of lax commitment—
neglecting my offerings and invocations.

O vajra brothers and sisters of body, speech, and mind
mandala deities solitary and in union,
I repent any insults caused by my jealousy:
I've discarded the gold flowers of affection and love.

I repent and cleanse any slippage
in my vow of individual liberation,
bodhisattva vow and mantra vow,
caused by omissions or weakness,
or by simple failing of mindfulness.

I repent searching the ultimate elsewhere;
I repent grasping the conventional as real;
I repent letting evil roam free;
I repent reifying compassion;
I repent seeking personal freedom;
I repent placing hopes in the ephemeral;
I repent reflecting on union with no discernment;
I repent without anything to repent for;
I repent with no one to do the repenting;
I repent without an object of repentance;
I repent seeking no fruits of repentance;
I repent making concrete whatever I see.

A Long Song of Sadness

Chone Lama Rinpoche (b. 1816)

I prostrate to noble Chenrezik and seek refuge in him.

The diamond nature of the actions of sages infinite as the ocean,
manifest in a dancing form adorned with saffron robes—
O my guru, your kindness is beyond return.
Place your feet in the dharma circle at my heart.

The demon of death, who eats the life and breath of beings
born in the vast forest of the three realms,
pursues them from the moment of their birth;
bless me, guru, so that I remember this.

Bees, little tigers performing a musical dance,
sucking the honey of beautiful flowers,
beware! The dewdrops of changing seasons
are not far away. They will strike soon.

O Suddhisara, absorbed in the tunes of dialectics
and persevering through studies in centers of logic,
beware! The last bead in your breath's rosary,
strung through night and day, may soon be clicked.

O beasts of the forest, whose darting glances spring from narrow
    eyes,
freely roaming the gray rocky mountains,
beware! Ill-meaning hunters surround you
quietly and take aim through their sights.

O Suddhisara, attached to the study of words and concepts
in the monastery of Tashi Khyil, seat of exposition and practice,
beware! How can you attain permanent joy
if even this place lies in the fangs of impermanence?

Birds singing tunes in the luxuriant garden
of full-bloom pipal trees, beware! The falcons
whose temperaments are dictated by karma
watch out for you, their vulnerable prey.

O Suddhisara, engaged in discourse with mind discerning
the meanings of scriptures at this center of knowledge,
beware! Be not deceived by superficial tasks;
you're caught in the jaws of the monster, impermanence.

Fish with white bellies and golden eyes,
swimming with agility in the vast turquoise lake,
beware! Fishermen are hiding at the water's edge
and holding rods with iron hooks.

O Suddhisara, proud of your powers in logic
at Tashi Khyil, where reason glows like a flame,
beware! The death demon constantly wielding
his weapon may strike at any time.

Merchants gathered at a marketplace, you have sold your
        dharma jewel,
the source of permanent joy, in exchange for pebbles,
mere worldly gains, yet are proud of the illusion of profit.
Return home soon! Remember your true purpose!

If you wish to attain the state of true learning
that directs your mind toward the ultimate goal,

discard your attachment to words and concepts
and observe the fluctuations of your mind.

Beware the childlike manner of walking, the mind
that has gone astray—mad in the dance of eight worldly concerns
and edging ever closer to the deep gorge of rebirth.
All manner of thorns afflict body and mind.

Your mind will wander in the long gorges of bardo,
when sickness destroys the friendship of body and mind,
your cherished carcass is carried to a charnel ground
and left naked on the soil before all eyes.

Look at the courage of so-called heroes who never shudder,
even when all the conditions are gathered
to dance for aeons on the burning iron ground,
and drink the hell fluids of melted bronze.

Though I have befriended the stainless scriptures
and learned their commentaries for a long time,
my mind remains hard as a pebble in water.
Beware the misfortune of an untamed mind: strive in virtue!

All the vivid appearance of the world and its beings,
not created by time, God, or a primal substance,
are but creative illusions of the mind, good old Brahma;
place your hope nowhere but in your mind alone.

I have wasted childhood, adolescence, manhood—
this rebirth of freedom and potential, so difficult to obtain,
like a wish-granting gem; if the kindness of the Three Jewels
grant me long life, may at least my old age be meaningful.

Let this childish mind, caught in senseless games,
attracted to the flowers of five senses,
stop the act of climbing and descending
the mountains and valleys of cyclic existence.
Tread now the precious staircase to supreme freedom.

Pay Heed, Pay Heed, O Zemey Tulku!

Zemey Lobsang Palden (1927–1996)

As I cast this hook of a few words
bearing messages of self-motivation,
pay heed, pay heed, O Zemey Tulku!
Contemplate from the depths of your heart.

Having entered the order, you carry the label
"a man who upholds the doctrine,"
and though you have the air of a learned scholar,
the chain of attachment to worldly concerns—
fruitless and futile—binds you ever tighter.

Oh no! Oh no! Refrain from evil deeds
with insight and deep commitment.
Always must you keep pure conduct,
always examine ill and good.

A monk's appearance gives a good impression;
internally you are lax in meditation:
you excel in the secret paths of sleep and distraction.
O my guru, behold this unfortunate fate.

When I look at others, my friends high and low,
and if I focus with a critical mind,
I am aware how futile are pursuits,
like the layers of a coreless banana tree.
Be not fooled seeing essence where there is none.

Pity those "brave" and "clever" young men
who lack any thought of an afterlife
and envy the sexual abandon of the monkeys. . . .
Oh, those foolish people!

Pity those "brave" and "clever" young men
who surrender even their lives
for good food, comfort, and fame.
Immutable as a diamond seem such habits!

Oh dear! Oh dear! Pray listen to me,
O Shakyamuni, our dear master.
Pity those who foster hatred,
who slander the upholders of dharma.

From within, it is besieged by corruption and deception;
from without, it is destroyed by military force.
What we still know as dharma now
looks like a patient on death's table.

Today your teachings, Shakyamuni Buddha,
may have a life span not longer than my end;
the world might yet see the demise of the dharma,
for its value lies beyond a cynical generation.

A Spring Day

Kelsang Gyatso, seventh Dalai Lama (1708–1757)

Supreme guru, primordial Buddha incarnate,
treasurer of the great way, voice of its secrets,
true refuge embodying the Three Jewels,
come, dwell in the lotus pool at my heart.

On the eighth day of a spring month,
in a time called the white year,
I tried to hold my mind and make it still—
my mind that wanders aimlessly.
Repeatedly I tried, ever more dejectedly.
I wished to merge my mind
in the sky of unstained space;
I wished to float my body
lightly, in dancing clouds.
Like a breeze in the open air,
my mind yearns to drift, ill at ease in rest.
Yet now, before the sun turns red and sets,
may I leave this place, this gaping state—
a field of lotus groves, spacious, blissful,
a mind at ease and joyful . . .

The busy chores of thought and action fail
to stem the surge of yearning from my heart.

Glossary and Notes on the Poems

All cross-references appear in small capitals. The abbreviation "Tib." stands for Tibetan and "San." for Sanskrit.

AFTERSESSIONS Refers to the periods between meditation sessions. In Tibetan contemplative traditions, meditators structure their daily spiritual practice around four sitting sessions, the first period starting in the early morning, around 4:00 AM, and the last one ending around 10:30 PM. The significance of calling the periods between meditation sessions "aftersessions" is to underline the crucial importance of maintaining the momentum of one's meditation practice even outside the formal sitting sessions.

AMDO (Tib.) The northeastern region of Tibet and one of the three provinces that constituted the old Tibet, the other two being Kham (eastern Tibet) and Ü-Tsang (central, southern, and western Tibet).

ANANDA (San.) Ananda was the principal attendant of the historical BUDDHA Shakyamuni (who died in the fifth century BCE) and was thus his constant companion. He is said to have heard every one of the Buddha's spoken teachings, and he played a crucial role in the recording of the Buddha's discourses following the latter's death. In "Wielding a Club in the Darkness," Tsangpa Gyare uses Ananda's life to exemplify the merits of possessing a vast scriptural knowledge as a spiritual resource.

AVALOKITESHVARA (San.) See CHENREZIK.

BARDO (Tib.) According to Buddhism, the fundamental pattern of our existence is a never-ending cycle of birth, death, and rebirth—known as SAMSARA, the perpetual cycle of unenlightened existence. This triad is interwoven with bardo, "intermediate" states of existence, during which it is believed that the being remains within a realm of reality that is devoid of corporeal existence. This so-called intermediate state is characterized by hallucinations, fluctuating levels of consciousness, fear, and uncertainties, all indicative of the profound transformation the being undergoes in this critical passage of the life cycle.

Though frightening for the ordinary being, for the spiritual adept the bardo is said to provide a rare opportunity to gain profound insight into the deeper nature of reality, as consciousness in this realm is believed to be free of the grosser levels of thought and sensory perception. Because of this, the Tibetan mystical tradition has developed specific meditation practices aimed at utilizing the consciousness of the intermediate state as part of the spiritual path. The Tibetan concept of bardo and its associated beliefs, especially according to the NYINGMA school of Tibetan Buddhism, is minutely recorded in the *Tibetan Book of the Dead*.

BENGUNG GYALPO (Tib.)   Possibly a reference to a legendary Tibetan meditator who is said to have totally transcended all worldly considerations.

BODHICHITTA (San.)   There are two levels of meaning to *bodhichitta*, literally, "the mind of awakening." In the conventional sense, it refers to a MAHAYANA ideal whereby the religious practitioner seeks to attain the highest enlightenment for the benefit of all sentient beings. In this sense, it is the highest expression of altruism in Mahayana Buddhism and is grounded in universal compassion. The one who has developed such a mind is called BODHISATTVA, the BUDDHA to be. The ultimate dimension of this altruistic mind is said to be the direct, unmediated experience of the nonsubstantiality of all things and events, especially the state of enlightenment itself, which is its object of aspiration. The two aspects of the awakening mind are called conventional bodhichitta and ultimate bodhichitta.

In esoteric Buddhism, however, there is a mystical level of meaning to the concept of bodhichitta. In this context, the "mind of awakening" refers to vital energy fluids that are activated within the practitioner's energy channels as a result of bliss-inducing meditation practices. The flow of such fluids is often described as kunda drops (for example, in "On the Inner Practice of Secret Mantra" by Drakpa Gyaltsen), implying that they are the basis of the profoundly blissful, sexual experiences associated with the meditations and visualizations of Kundalini yoga.

BODHISATTVA (San.)   An important concept in MAHAYANA Buddhism. A bodhisattva (literally "the one who aspires to full enlightenment") is a spiritual aspirant who lives according to an altruistic pledge made when he or she first generated BODHICHITTA: the pledge to attain Buddhahood for the sake of all sentient beings—to forgo one's own liberation until all beings are saved. For the devout, the bodhisattva principle represents the heroic ideals of self-sacrifice, boundless tolerance, universal compassion, and the perfect harmony of insight and empathy.

BRAHMA (San.)   In ancient Indian mythology, Brahma is the creator of the universe and is depicted as a deity with four heads. However, the term Brahma is often also used to connote purity and the pristine nature of things.

BUDDHA (San.)   Throughout the poems, "Buddha" is used as a generic name referring to someone who is believed to have attained full awakening. When referring to the historical Buddha, the Tibetan writers often add Shakyamuni, the personal name by which the historical Buddha (who died in the fifth century BCE) is known to his followers. Thus, one can speak of "the Buddha of compassion," "the Buddha of wisdom," and so forth, and one can also understand the myth of the thousand Buddhas. According to this myth, Shakyamuni is the fourth Buddha, and the fifth will be the future Buddha, Maitreya.

BUDDHA SAMDRUP (Tib.)   A reference to a personal teacher of Karma Trinley's, who was called Samdrup. It is quite customary in the Tibetan tradition to refer to one's guru as a Buddha, "the enlightened one."

BUDDHA'S FOUR BODIES   See FOUR KAYAS.

CHAKRAS (San.)   In VAJRAYANA Buddhism, *chakras* refers to energy centers at critical points of a person's body. Formed by two side energy channels looping around a central channel at various points, and various smaller channels branching off from these junctures, the principal chakras, or "wheels," are said to be located at the crown of the head, the throat, the heart, the navel, and the base of the sexual organs. According to Tibetan mystical teachings, these chakras are believed to be important bases of vital forces such as bliss, visionary experience, and levels of physical and mental isolations, or ego-free states of realization. In this view, it is the flowing of "winds" and VITAL DROPS within these channels that gives rise to profound states of experience. Of these chakras, the heart chakra is considered to be the most important center of energy and is often metaphorically described in the shape of an eight-petaled lotus. So, when poets supplicate their GURU to place his feet in their heart (for example, Chone Lama Rinpoche in "Movements of Dancing Lightning"), they are actually asking the guru to enter the heart chakra and induce the experience of bliss to arise spontaneously.

CHAKRASAMVARA (San.)   An important "meditation DEITY" in esoteric Buddhism representing the "transmutation" of the energy of desire. Chakrasamvara (literally "binding of all things together as a single circle of deities") symbolizes the idea of unification of the entire expanse of reality within the sphere of one's experience of mystic consciousness. He is often depicted in sexual union with his consort Varahi, the union representing the nonduality of wisdom and compassion—that is, the feminine and the masculine. There are many different aspects of this meditation deity derived from the various lineages initiated by the great Indian mystics who dedicated their spiritual practice to this important tradition. Chakrasamvara is also known as Heruka, the "blood-drinker," the redness of blood signifying the enlightened consummation of the passions. For the mystic, meditation deities like Chakrasamvara represent the archetype through which he or she attains a union of self with the GURU, the meditation deity, and the entire universe. This is the sense in which Chone Lama invokes his guru in "A Vajra Song Aspiring to Tread the Footsteps of the Heroes" when he writes "O guru Heruka, . . ."

CHANDRAKIRTI (ca. seventh century CE)   An important figure in the history of Buddhist philosophy, especially the MADHYAMAKA school of MAHAYANA Buddhism. The Tibetan tradition accredits Chandrakirti with the founding of the PRASANGIKA division of the Madhyamaka school following his novel interpretation of the EMPTINESS philosophy of NAGARJUNA (ca. second century CE). All four schools of Tibetan Buddhism see Chandrakirti's Prasangika school as representing the apex of Buddhist philosophical thinking. See, for example, "Recognizing My Mother" by Changkya.

CHANNELS   Refers to energy pathways that are believed to pervade the entire human body, according to esoteric Buddhism. See also CHAKRAS.

CHENREZIK (Tib.)   The BUDDHA of compassion, arguably the most important religious figure in Tibetan Buddhism. Tibetans regard Chenrezik (Avalokiteshvara in Sanskrit) as their patron deity and believe that he has made a special pledge to protect the well-being of the people of the "land of snows." Because of this, the Tibetans consider many of their great rulers of the past to have been emanations of Chenrezik, for example, the successive Dalai Lamas. There are many different aspects of Chenrezik, the most famous being the thousand-armed Buddha of compassion. Interestingly, figures such as Chenrezik (compassion), Manjushri (wisdom), Tara (action), and Vajrapani (power) display a complex interplay of history, myth, and religion in the life of a devout practitioner. Chenrezik is a "historical" figure in that he is a BODHISATTVA who was a disciple of the Buddha as described in the MAHAYANA scriptures. As the Buddha of compassion, he is also the embodiment of the compassion of all the Buddhas (the fully enlightened ones). Yet he is also an archetype in that he represents the perfected state of the practitioner's own natural compassion.

COMPLETION STAGE   One of the two stages—the other being the "generation stage"—in the levels of realization according to the Highest Yoga class of VAJRAYANA Buddhism. Generation stage is characterized by "simulation," where the practitioner's engagement in the path involves predominantly contrived states of meditation. These include, among others, the visualization and identification of oneself with a chosen meditation deity such as CHAKRASAMVARA, and simulating experiences of great bliss. In contrast, when the wisdom of emptiness, which is in union with great bliss, becomes part of the practitioner's actual reality, he or she is then said to have reached the completion stage.

DAKINIS (San.)   Literally meaning "space voyager"—that is, someone who is immersed in the profound experience of the ultimate expanse of reality—a dakini is a female representation of the enlightened mind. Often wrathful, at times playful, she is the heroine within. A dakini can also be a woman mystic who has attained high levels of realization and is thus said to be an appropriate partner for a male mystic on the path to enlightenment. Corresponding to the levels of their meditative realization, there are said to be different types of dakinis, such as the field-born and the mantra-born. This dakini principle underlines the need for the inseparability of the male and female energies for full awakening.

DEITY   Throughout the poems, *deity* is used as a generic term to refer to "divine" representations visualized in a meditator's transformed states of consciousness. In a strict sense, a deity is nothing but the archetypal symbol of the perfected state of the meditator's own mind. In Tibetan Buddhism, the concept of the meditation deity is an essential element of the religious practice, as the identification of one's own mind with the GURU and one's meditation deity constitutes the core of a daily meditation. For an example of one such deity, see CHAKRASAMVARA.

DEPENDENT ORIGINATION   One of the most important concepts of Buddhist philosophy and intimately connected with the Buddhist understanding of the laws of causality. The Sanskrit word for dependent origination is *pratityasamutpada*, which literally means "that which arises through dependence and relatedness." The notion of dependent origination can be seen in its most developed form in the MIDDLE WAY (see also NAGARJUNA) doctrine of EMPTINESS, especially in the PRASANGIKA's equation of emptiness with dependent origination. In this view, dependence is understood in terms of the mere conditionality of things and events and thus implies the absence of any independent mode of being. So, emptiness and dependent origination become two dimensions—the ultimate and the relative—of one and the same world. This way of understanding the nature of reality in terms of profound interdependence became dominant in Tibet following the influence of Tsongkhapa's philosophical writings. For poets and philosophers alike, it is the concept of dependent origination that holds the key to understanding the diversity, complexity, and a certain element of uniformity in the natural world. In their quest for insight, the poets and philosophers evoke notions such as dependent aggregation, codependent arising, mutual dependence, the dependent world, and dependent nature. Changkya's long poem called "Recognizing My Mother" begins with a fascinating play between emptiness and dependent origination through the metaphor of a child's interplay with his parents. See also "Reflections on Emptiness," "In Praise of the Vision of Father Lobsang," "Ramblings of a Drunken Bee," "A Spontaneous Song Evoked by the Dream-Girl," "Melodies of an Echo," and "The Love Dance of Emptiness and Appearance."

DHARMA (San.)   Broadly meaning "custom," "duty," "law," or "religion," *dharma* refers to a pattern or a set of patterns that govern human thought and behavior. In the Buddhist context, however, *dharma* is used to refer to the scriptural teachings of the BUDDHA and the levels of realization that are derived on the basis of the practice of these teachings. Along with the Buddha and the sangha, the spiritual community, dharma is an object of refuge. Together, these three are known as the THREE JEWELS.

DHARMAKAYA (San.) In MAHAYANA Buddhism, the full awakening of Buddhahood is characterized in terms of three "embodiments" known as kayas (literally, "bodies"). Dharmakaya, or "truth body," is both the ultimate nature of the enlightened mind and the ultimate expanse of existence. *Sambhogakaya*, or "the buddha body of perfect resource," is the natural expression of the enlightened mind in its primordial form, radiant, spontaneous, and beyond materiality. *Nirmanakaya*, or "emanation body," is the manifestation of this primordial form in its physical embodiments within the realm of diversity and multiplicity. In many of the poems we find dharmakaya as the natural "abode" of the fully enlightened ones, and the poet calls upon the BUDDHAS to appear from within this expanse (for example, "On the Death of Kyabje Trijhang Rinpoche" by Zemey Lobsang Palden). In esoteric Buddhism, various meditations have been devised that involve correlating these three enlightened embodiments with death, the intermediate state, and rebirth. Viewed thus, the three kayas become a metaphor for the fundamental cycle of life whereby every event goes through the never-ending process of death, intermediate state, and rebirth.

DHARMODGATA (San.) A name of a BODHISATTVA and the teacher of Sadaprarudita in a popular story of MAHAYANA Buddhism. According to the story, Sadaprarudita once heard a voice from the sky admonishing him to seek Dharmodgata and receive the sacred "perfection of wisdom" teachings from him. The long search for his teacher, the trials to which Sadaprarudita was subjected by the god Indra, the manner in which Sadaprarudita's single-pointed dedication impressed many daughters of the powerful merchant families, and the culmination of the story in Sadaprarudita's meeting with Dharmodgata remain to this day a source of inspiration to many devout Mahayana Buddhists. In Tibetan Buddhism, this story is seen as exemplary of the ideal way in which the practitioner must revere his or her spiritual mentor. See, for example, Tsongkhapa's "Prayer for the Flourishing of Virtues."

DHIH The seed syllable of Manjushri, the Buddha of wisdom. In "A Dance of Unwavering Devotion," Chone Lama uses it to refer to a syllable of his personal name in Sanskrit, which he writes as Suddhisara.

DO-ME (Tib.) Another name for AMDO.

DOORS OF BODY, SPEECH, AND MIND   These three are sometimes referred to as the "three doors," indicating that it is through our body, speech,
and mind that all our actions emanate.

DUHKHA (San.)   Translated often as "suffering," *duhkha* refers to the fun-
damentally unsatisfying nature of conditioned existence according to Buddhism. It is the very fact of our existence as unenlightened, devoid of freedom,
and controlled by powerful forces of delusion and negative impulses.

EASTERN MASTERS   Bhavaviveka, Shantarakshita, and Kamalashila, who
are the three main thinkers of the Svatantrika-Madhyamaka school of classical
Indian Buddhism. Although these masters subscribed to the basic tenets of
the MIDDLE WAY philosophy of NAGARJUNA, they were said to maintain a
belief in some notion of intrinsic existence. In other words, these interpreters
of Nagarjuna shied away from the thoroughgoing nominalism of thinkers such
as Buddhapalita and CHANDRAKIRTI.

EIGHT PLEAS   In "On How to Engage in a Meditative Path," Drakpa Gyaltsen ends his song by asking the reader to pay heed to his eight pleas. This is
a reference to the appeals he had made in the poem (1) to give up concerns
for worldly goods, (2) to have compassion for all beings, (3) to honor enlightened beings, (4) not to be led astray by speculative views, (5) to go beyond
thought and language, (6) to transcend the dualism of "good" and "evil,"
(7) to eradicate all desires of endeavor, and (8) to enhance nonobjectifying
compassion.

EIGHT WORLDLY CONCERNS   Joyful when praised, unhappy when dis-
paraged; joyful when respected, unhappy when insulted; joyful when obtaining
material things, unhappy when not; joyful when in good health, unhappy when
not. These four sets of reactions are said to dominate the mind of an ordinary
person, chaining him or her to states of perpetual discontent. A spiritual
practitioner is encouraged to go beyond these habitual tendencies.

EMAHO! (Tib.)   A joyful exclamation akin to saying "Oh, what joy!"

EMPTINESS   According to Nagarjuna's Middle Way philosophy, the ultimate
truth of all phenomena is said to be emptiness, that is, the fact of their lack
of any independent, intrinsic, substantial reality. This is the philosophical
perspective that almost all the poets of our anthology share. In our translation

we have sometimes chosen either "void" or "voidness" as an alternative to "emptiness," although we remain conscious of the dangers of reification, especially with the usage of "the void." The choice is based solely on aesthetic and poetic sensibility to facilitate a smoother reading. See also DEPENDENT ORIGINATION, NAGARJUNA, and the MIDDLE WAY.

ESSENCE   Here often used as a translation of the Tibetan term *rangshin,* it is a shorthand way of referring to the ultimate nature of reality. According to its contexts, this epithet could mean "EMPTINESS"—the absence of intrinsic being—or, in the case of some of the poets included in the present volume, the term may have a more affirmative connotation.

E-VAM   A composite of two syllables, E-VAM is an important symbol of nonduality in VAJRAYANA Buddhism. It represents the nonduality of subject and object, in that E is the object EMPTINESS and VAM is the transcendental awareness that experiences it (for example, "On the Inner Practice of Secret Mantra"). This is synonymous with the nonduality of bliss and emptiness, in that a blissful consciousness is immersed in the truth of the emptiness of all things. It also represents the nonduality of body and mind in that it stands for the Buddha's perfect assimilation of matter into mind in his attainment of the state transcendent of corporeal existence.

FIELD-BORN DAKINIS   See DAKINIS.

FIVE POISONS   In addition to attachment, anger, and delusion (the three root poisons), the five poisons include deluded views and negative skepticism. In Buddhist psychological literature, these five mental states are also known as the "five root afflictions."

FIVE SENSE DOORS   The organs of the five senses, that is, eyes, ears, nose, tongue, and body, are sometimes called the five doors, implying that it is through these doorways that we engage with the sensual objects of the world.

"FOOT IN MY HEART"   See CHAKRAS.

FOUR DEMONS   Lust, death, delusion, and corporeal existence are said to be the four "demons" in that they obstruct an individual on his or her path to enlightenment. Full enlightenment is characterized by total freedom from these four obstructions. Machik's short song ("Cutting the Rope of Conceit") gives an account of the process of gaining victory over these demons.

FOUR IMPURE ELEMENTS   These refer to the practitioner's own internal elements of earth, water, fire, and air. They are "impure" in that they are the physical constituents of an unenlightened being and thus need to be transformed into the pure elements of an enlightened being.

FOUR JOYS   (1) Joy, (2) great joy, (3) extraordinary joy, and (4) simultaneously born joy. These relate to four stages in the experience of bliss engendered through the flow of VITAL DROPS in the context of the Highest Yoga path of VAJRAYANA Buddhism. They are associated respectively with the flow of vital drops from the crown to the throat, from the throat to the heart, from the heart to the navel, and finally, from the navel to the sexual organ. Thus the fourth joy is the apex and culmination of the overall blissful process.

FOUR KAYAS   Often the three kayas (see DHARMAKAYA) are described in terms of four. On this enumeration, dharmakaya is divided into its two dimensions, *svabhavikakaya*, that is, the "natural embodiment of the BUDDHA," and *jnanadharmakaya*, "wisdom truth body." The first refers to the ultimately empty nature of the enlightened mind, while the second refers to this mind itself.

FOUR PAIRED WORLDLY STAINS   The same as EIGHT WORLDLY CONCERNS.

FOUR SKILLFUL ACTIONS   (1) Pacification, (2) enrichment, (3) empowerment, and (4) wrath. These four approaches characterize the skillful means of an enlightened being when engaging in the altruistic activity of helping other sentient beings. First, peaceful means or methods of pacification are employed, gradually leading to the latter, progressively more forceful means of persuasion.

FOURFOLD REASONING   This refers to four avenues of investigation into the nature of reality based on what Buddhist philosophy characterizes as the four principles of nature (see, for example, "A Prayer for the Flourishing of Virtues" by Tsongkhapa). They are the principle (1) of nature, (2) of dependence, (3) of function, and (4) of logical inference. Briefly stated, the first principle relates to the fundamental nature of things, the way things really are at their most basic level. The second principle relates to the nature of dependence that exists in reality, such as between the causes and effects and so on. The third principle relates to specific functions that individual elements possess, and more importantly, the functions that arise from their aggregations. Finally, the fourth principle relates to the laws of logical evidence that can be utilized on the basis of understanding all three preceding principles of nature.

GARUDA (San.)   The mythical bird ridden by the god Vishnu. Garuda is also the enemy of serpents in Indian mythology. Tibetan poets often use the imagery of Garuda to evoke a sense of loftiness and of the cruising skills that describe the qualities of heightened meditative states of mind.

GELUK (Tib.)   Founded by the great religious reformer of Tibet, Tsongkhapa (1357–1419), Geluk is the newest of the four main schools of Tibetan Buddhism. The school derives its name from Ganden, a monastery established by Tsongkhapa in 1409 near LHASA. Ganden was soon followed by the establishment of two other large monasteries, Drepung in 1415 and Sera in 1419; together the three monasteries became great centers of learning in central Tibet until 1959, when the Chinese occupation of Tibet led to the flight of the Dalai Lama and thousands of Tibetans into exile. With the assumption of political power by the fifth Dalai Lama in the seventeenth century, Geluk became the ruling school in Tibet.

GENERATION STAGE   The first of the two stages (the other being COMPLETION STAGE) that constitute the levels of attainment in VAJRAYANA Buddhism according to the Tibetan tradition.

GESHE (Tib.)   Literally meaning "spiritual friend," *Geshe* gradually came to signify a specific academic association. Today, in its popular usage, it refers to an academic title that can be equated with a doctorate in divinity. The highest form of the Geshe title is Lharam, the holder of which is a graduate of a major monastic university who has accomplished the study of the five primary topics of academic discourse: (1) logic and epistemology, (2) MAHAYANA religious studies, (3) the MIDDLE WAY philosophy, (4) Buddhist psychology and phenomenology, and (5) Buddhist ethics. See, for example, Gungthang's "Ramblings of an Aged Man."

GREAT PERFECTION   See ZOKCHEN.

GREAT PERFECTION HEART DROPS   A specific lineage of ZOKCHEN teachings called heart drops evolved in the eighteenth century following the revelation of important texts by the NYINGMA master Jigme Lingpa (1729–1788). However, in "An Adamantine Song on Purposeless Pursuits," Longchen Rabjampa is using the epithet to refer to the essence of Zokchen teachings as a whole.

GREAT SEAL   See MAHAMUDRA.

GREAT VEHICLE   See MAHAYANA.

GREAT WAY   The same as the Great Vehicle and MAHAYANA.

GURU (San.)   A teacher, mentor, or spiritual guide. The concept of guru is important in Tibetan Buddhism, since a successful spiritual realization takes place within the context of Guru Yoga, which involves identifying the guru and meditation DEITY with the practitioner's own mind. It is said that the guru is the source of all blessings; the meditation deities are the source of powerful attainments; the DAKINIS and protectors are the source of safety and the overcoming of obstacles. A successful religious practice must be based on a sound relationship with one's guru. Many of the poets in the present collection invoke the blessing of their guru at the beginning of their songs of spiritual awakening.

HAM   A seed syllable of a Sanskrit MANTRA; it is often visualized at the navel in certain esoteric meditation practices. For example, in "At the Feet of the Lord of Dance," Karma Trinley invokes the meditation DEITY CHAKRASAMVARA in the form of the letter HAM.

HEAT GENERATION   A form of practice belonging to the esoteric tradition that involves generation of heat within the body through meditation.

HERUKA (San.)   See CHAKRASAMVARA.

IMMORTAL DIAMOND BODY   An epithet of an enlightened embodiment where the individual is said to be beyond death. This is the sense in which the seventh Dalai Lama uses the epithet in "Inspire Me to Remember Death." See also FOUR KAYAS.

INNER, OUTER, AND SECRET DEEDS   "Inner deeds" refers to operations of the mind, especially the levels of realization, "outer deeds" to external behavior, where actions can be observed and judged by conventional standards, and "secret deeds" suggests activities that may have a mysterious significance or cannot be judged in conventional terms. See, for example, "Movements of Dancing Lightning" by Chone Lama Rinpoche.

"INSTRUCTIONS SENT THROUGH THE WIND" A poetic expression indicating that the precious instructions of one's teachers came through a transmission of an unbroken lineage of masters.

JEWELS   See THREE JEWELS.

JHANGCHUP SHÖNU   Name of a person, possibly an important student of the poet, referred to in "Wielding a Club in the Darkness" by Tsangpa Gyare.

KAGYÜ (Tib.)   One of the four main schools of Tibetan Buddhism, the Kagyü tradition was founded by Marpa Lotsawa (1012–1097), the great poet mystic Milarepa (1040–1123), and Gampopa (1079–1153) in the eleventh century. One of the most important institutions of the Kagyü school is the successive lineages of Karmapas (for example, Rangjung Dorje in the present collection). The Kagyü school emphasizes the approach of MAHAMUDRA in its meditative practice.

KARMA (San.)   The concept of karma is fundamental to moral philosophy in both Buddhist and Hindu thinking. *Karma* can mean an individual act, or it can also mean the whole mechanism of cause and effect. According to the theory of karma, there is a commensurability between an act and its consequences: virtuous acts lead to happiness and nonvirtuous ones to suffering (for example, "A Song of Self-Encouragement toward True Renunciation" by Chone Lama Rinpoche). The twin axioms of the concept of karma are that no one experiences effects of deeds not done, and a deed once done never loses its potency for creating its corresponding effects.

KARMA LHALONG   Name of a retreat.

KARMAPA (Tib.)   The highest ranking lama in the KAGYÜ school of Tibetan Buddhism. Like the successive Dalai Lamas, the succession of Karmapa is based on the Tibetan tradition of recognizing the "reincarnation" of the deceased predecessor. In fact, it is with the formal recognition of Karmapa Pakshi (1204–1283) as the reincarnation of Karmapa Düsum Khyenpa at the turn of the thirteenth century that the institution of reincarnate lamas began in Tibetan Buddhism.

KHENCHEN NGAGI WANGPO   "He (or she) who is perfect in speech." Ngagi Wangpo is an epithet often used to refer to Manjushri, the BUDDHA of wisdom. Because of the association of speech with transcendent wisdom, sometimes poets also refer to their guru as "one who is perfect in speech." (However, in "A Song of Self-Encouragement toward True Renunciation," by Chone Lama Rinpoche, the poet is actually referring to one of his teachers whose first name is Ngawang, which is an abbreviation of Ngagi Wangpo.) *Khenchen* means the "great abbot."

KING CHANDRAPRABHA   Possibly a reference to one of the former lives of the BUDDHA as told in the *Jataka Tales*, classical stories that describe the previous incarnations of the Buddha.

KUNDA (San.)   See BODHICHITTA.

KUNTU SANGPO (Tib.)   Known as Samantabhadra in Sanskrit, Kuntu Sangpo is the name of the primordial BUDDHA according to the NYINGMA teachings. He is characterized as the ever-present, ever-pure, primordially enlightened being; he is the source of all the multiplicity of the world of experience. In brief, he is the DHARMAKAYA embodiment of all the Buddhas. See "A Sky with a Center and Borders!" and "An Adamantine Song on Purposeless Pursuits" by Longchen Rabjampa.

LHASA   The capital city of Tibet where the famous seventh-century Potala palace is located.

LOBSANG DRAKPA   The personal name of Tsongkhapa (1357–1419), the great fourteenth-century religious reformer and one of Tibet's foremost philosophers. Tsongkhapa is seen by historians as the founder of the GELUK school of Tibetan Buddhism.

LOBSANG VICTOR   See LOBSANG DRAKPA.

LORD OF DEATH   See YAMA

MADHYAMAKA (San.)   See MIDDLE WAY.

MADHYAMIKA (San.)   A follower of the MIDDLE WAY (Madhyamaka) school of Indian MAHAYANA Buddhism. See also MIDDLE WAY and NAGARJUNA .

MAHAMUDRA (San.) Literally meaning the "great seal," *mahamudra* has several different meanings. It can refer to the experience of EMPTINESS, the all-encompassing ultimate nature of reality, or it can refer to the highest state of enlightenment. In both these contexts, the "seal" has the sense of the highest authority or a limit that cannot be transgressed. (See "Laying the Ground for Forbearance" by Rangjung Dorje.) Often, *mahamudra* is used also to signify a specific set of highly advanced meditation practices that involve taking the nature of one's own mind as the focus.

MAHASIDDHA (San.) A term used in Buddhist literature to refer to a great mystic. The word is derived from *siddhi*, "powerful attainments," and implies an individual who has gained high levels of realization. Mahasiddhas are often colorful characters who are capable of transcending the strictures of worldly customs and conventions, and who often write their profound mystical insights in the form of songs. (See "Old Dog in the Wilderness" by Za Paltrül.) The Tibetan tradition recounts eighty-four great mahasiddhas of India, which include among others the great Tilopa, the master of NAROPA, and Saraha, the author of the mystical songs known as *dohas*.

MAHAYANA (San.) Literally the "Great Vehicle," *Mahayana* refers to one of the two main trends of Buddhism (the other being Hinayana, or "Lesser Vehicle"). This is the form of Buddhism that flourished in Tibet, China, Japan, Korea, and Vietnam. The principal feature of Mahayana is the so-called BODHISATTVA ideal whereby the religious virtuoso takes the liberation of all sentient beings as his or her principal spiritual goal.

MANDALA (San.) A "circle," "wheel," "circumference," or "totality," a mandala is a cosmic symbol of the universe often depicted in concentric, symmetric patterns. Such symbols are employed in esoteric Buddhism to visualize the meditator's own states of consciousness in the form of celestial abodes and deities (see DEITY) residing within them.

MANDALA GODS Refers to meditation deities (see DEITY) visualized within a MANDALA circle.

MANJUSHRI (San.) The Buddha of wisdom. See also CHENREZIK.

MANTRA A sacred ritual formula composed from a combination of several syllables of Sanskrit. OM MANI PADME HUM, the six-syllable mantra of CHEN-

REZIK, the BUDDHA of compassion, is the most famous example. Often the mantras are like mnemonic symbols and may not have any literal meaning in the sense of a conventional sentence.

MANTRA-BORN DAKINIS   See DAKINIS.

MARA (San.)   Often translated as "demon," *mara* refers to certain obstructive forces as recognized in the Buddhist texts. There are four principal maras or malevolent forces: the mara (1) of death, (2) of mental afflictions, (3) of desire, and (4) of conditioned existence. The overcoming of all of these maras constitutes the attainment of full enlightenment. In classical Buddhist literature, the Buddha is described as having conquered the maras by his powers of loving-kindness and compassion.

MARPA   Marpa Lotsawa (1012–1097), who came from the region of Lhodrak in Tibet, was a great translator of the Indian Buddhist scriptures into Tibetan and the master of Milarepa, Tibet's most-loved religious personality. (See "Biographies of the Poets" on the life of Milarepa.) Marpa studied under the Indian pandit NAROPA, who, together with Tilopa, is seen by the KAGYÜ tradition as the principal source of its lineage.

MIDDLE PATH   See MADHYAMIKA and NAGARJUNA.

MIDDLE WAY   All classical Indian Buddhist philosophical schools characterize their standpoints as representing the true middle way—transcending the extremes of absolutism and nihilism. However, the epithet Madhyamaka (Middle Way) later became primarily associated with NAGARJUNA's (ca. second century CE) philosophy of EMPTINESS. On this view, all beliefs in the objective, intrinsic reality of the self and the world are rejected, and the absolute negation of intrinsic existence, which is described as emptiness, is recognized as representing the ultimate truth about things and events. Nagarjuna's key work outlining his theory of emptiness is the *Fundamentals of the Middle Way,* where he subjects all aspects of reality, including cause and effect, subject and object, self and the world, to minute analysis, thereby deconstructing any notion of intrinsic identity and existence.

MILAREPA   See "Biographies of the Poets."

MOUNT KAILASH   A holy mountain in the Himalayan range in western Tibet. This mountain is sacred to both Buddhists and Hindus. For the Buddhists, it is associated with CHAKRASAMVARA, while for the Hindus, it is the abode of the god Shiva. In Tibetan poetry, Mount Kailash is often used as an archetype of all snow mountains and works as a metaphor for purity, the source, and towering intellect. (For example, "On the Death of Kyabje Tri-jhang Rinpoche" by Zemey Lobsang Palden.)

NAGARJUNA (ca. second century CE)   Undisputedly one of the greatest thinkers in Buddhist history, Nagarjuna is regarded by historians as the founder of the MIDDLE WAY school of Buddhism. His philosophy of EMPTI-NESS and the nonsubstantiality of all things became the dominant current in Buddhist thought, attracting followers of such towering intellect as Bhavavi-veka, CHANDRAKIRTI, and Shantideva. The Tibetan tradition considers Nagar-juna to be one of the two most important figures in the history of Indian MAHAYANA Buddhism (the other being Asanga). Nagarjuna's most important work is his *Fundamentals of the Middle Way*.

NAROPA (1016–1100)   An accomplished Buddhist thinker from Nalanda monastery in central India, Naropa later became a YOGIN and a pupil of the MAHASIDDHA Tilopa. Naropa is revered in the Tibetan tradition as the master of MARPA Lotsawa and also the progenitor of a highly sophisticated set of tantric meditative practices (see SUTRA) known as the "six yogas of Naropa."

NGAWANG   The first name of one of Chone Lama's principal teachers, whose blessings are invoked at the beginning of "Melodies of an Echo."

NIRVANA (San.)   Literally meaning "beyond sorrow," *nirvana* refers to the Buddhist notion of liberation. Nirvana as the attainment of enlightenment is often contrasted with SAMSARA, that is, unenlightened existence characterized by the never-ending cycle of birth and death. See, for example, "Reflections on Emptiness" and "A Sky with a Center and Borders!" by Tsongkhapa and Longchen Rabjampa, respectively.

NYINGMA (Tib.)   The oldest of the four main schools of Tibetan Bud-dhism, the Nyingma school came into being as a result of a large-scale system-atic attempt to establish Buddhism as the official religion of Tibet between the eighth and ninth centuries. The key figures involved in this endeavor were the monarch Trisong Detsen, the Indian scholar Shantarakshita, and the mys-tic Padmasambhava. A principal feature of the Nyingma tradition is its empha-sis on the "revealed tradition," a highly developed textual hermeneutics based on the idea of hidden treasure texts. The school also has a sophisticated set of practices and their underlying theories enshrined in a systematic approach known as ZOKCHEN, the Great Perfection.

PITH INSTRUCTIONS   In the Tibetan contemplative tradition there is a concept of a special set or sets of teachings imparted from a GURU to his or her pupil. Such teachings are said to constitute "pith instructions" in that they represent the extracted essence of all the scriptures processed and refined on the basis of the guru's own direct, personal experience of the profound truth. This notion is particularly dominant in the KAGYÜ and NYINGMA schools of Tibetan Buddhism.

PRASANGIKA (San.)   A school of classical Indian Buddhist philosophy evolved from a unique interpretation of NAGARJUNA's philosophy of EMPTI- NESS. The key proponents of this school of thought were Buddhapalita (ca. fifth to sixth century), CHANDRAKIRTI (ca. seventh century), and Shantideva (ca. seventh century), the author of the well-known Mahayana classic *Guide to the Bodhisattva's Way of Life*. All four schools of Tibetan Buddhism recognize Prasangika as representing the apex of Buddhist philosophical thinking and characterize their own philosophical standpoints as being the true Prasangika position.

PRATITYASAMUTPADA (San.)   See DEPENDENT ORIGINATION.

RAHULA (San.)   According to Indian mythology, Rahula, or Rahu, is a demon who supposedly seizes sun and moon, thus causing their eclipse. This idea of Rahula's seizing the sun is often used as a metaphor in Tibetan poetry (for example, "On the Death of Kyabje Trijhang Rinpoche" by Zemey Lob- sang Palden).

RIKPA (Tib.)   Literally meaning "to know," *rikpa* is often used by the Ti- betan mystics, especially the practitioners of NYINGMA teachings, to mean "pure awareness" or "pristine cognition." In this sense, rikpa is a quality of innate mind that is fundamental and in its natural state spontaneous and pure. This notion of rikpa is especially dominant in the ZOKCHEN writings of the Nyingma school. See "An Adamantine Song on Purposeless Pursuits" and "An Adamantine Song on the Ever-Present" by Longchen Rabjampa.

RONG   A place in the northeastern part of Tibet. Kalden Gyatso, in "The Joys of the Solitary Hills," identifies Rong as his birthplace.

SADAPRARUDITA (San.)   See DHARMODGATA.

SAKYA (Tib.)   One of the four main schools of Tibetan Buddhism, the Sakya school came into being following Khön Könchok Gyalpo's founding of the Sakya monastery in 1073. At the beginning of the thirteenth century, when the great Sakya hierarch Kunga Gyaltsen (1182–1251) came into contact with the Mongol rulers, the Sakya school began to play an important role in the political history of Tibet. The nephew of Kunga Gyaltsen (also known as Sakya Pandita) nephew Chögyal Phakpa (1235–1280) became the de facto ruler of Tibet, making the Sakya school the principal political power in Tibet until the fifteenth century.

SAMADHI (San.)   A meditative state where the mind has reached a deep level of absorption and single-pointedness. See "A Response to a Logician" by Milarepa.

SAMANTABHADRA   See KUNTU SANGPO.

SAMSARA (San.)   A cycle of unenlightened existence constituted by the never-ending process of life and death. According to Buddhism, at the root of such unenlightened existence is a fundamental ignorance that gives rise to a whole process of delusion and a confused way of being in the world. This is contrasted with NIRVANA, "release" or "liberation," where the individual is said to have gained total freedom from suffering.

SAUTRANTIKA (San.)   One of the four classical Indian Buddhist philosophical schools, Sautrantika can be described as a Buddhist realist school. Its central tenets were that the physical world is made of substantially real atomic elements and that consciousness is constituted by indivisible units of cognitive factors. Epistemologically, the school posited an apperceptive faculty called self-cognition that was believed to be an essential feature of all cognitive events. In other words, Sautrantikas argued that when we are aware of something, that is, an object, the cognition is reflexively aware of itself too. Changkya, in his long poem on EMPTINESS ("Recognizing My Mother"), takes issue with the Sautrantika school for accepting a notion of the "intrinsic subject."

SHAKYAMUNI   See BUDDHA.

SHEPA DORJE   An epithet of the poet-saint Milarepa, one of the poets in our anthology. In "Movements of Dancing Lightning," however, Chone Lama may be referring to one of his own personal gurus.

SIX CYCLES   This refers to a specific set of six practices designed to help embrace all events of life as factors complementing and enhancing one's spiritual practice. This practice is particularly developed in the teachings of the KAGYÜ school of Tibetan Buddhism, where it is characterized as a practice that assimilates all "tastes" into one. The six cycles are: (1) taking conceptions into the path, (2) taking mental afflictions into the path, (3) taking sicknesses into the path, (4) taking gods and demons into the path, (5) taking sufferings into the path, and (6) taking death into the path. Drukpa Künlek evokes this idea of merging of all tastes in his "In Response to a Request for Teaching on Cause and Effect."

SIX MINDFULNESSES   The mindfulnesses of GURU, BUDDHA, DHARMA, spiritual community (*sangha*), moral discipline (*shila*), and generosity (*dana*).

SIX PERFECTIONS   (1) Generosity, (2) ethical discipline, (3) forbearance, (4) vigor, (5) concentration, and (6) wisdom or insight. Together, these six practices constitute the heart of the BODHISATTVA's endeavor toward his or her attainment of full enlightenment for the benefit of all beings. As such, these six perfections encapsulate the essence of the teachings and practice of MAHAYANA Buddhism.

SIX REALMS   According to Buddhist cosmology, after death, as long as they remain within an unenlightened existence, sentient beings take rebirth in any of the six realms (that is, human, celestial, demigod, animal, hungry ghost, and hell-like).

SIX SENSES   The five sense organs plus the mental organ, that is, the mind.

SIXFOLD CONSCIOUSNESS   The five sensory consciousnesses plus the mind.

SKANDHAS (San.)   Literally "aggregates," *skandhas* refers to psychological and physical elements that together constitute the existence and identity of a person in Buddhist thought. There are five such "aggregates," namely: body, feeling, perception, mental formations, and consciousness. In Buddhist discourse and meditation, the analysis of the nature of self and identity often takes the form of examining the relation between these aggregates and the "person." See "Awake from the Slumber of Ignorance!" by the seventh Dalai lama.

SUCHNESS   An epithet of EMPTINESS, the ultimate nature of reality.

SUDDHISARA   The Sanskrit version of Lodrö Gyatso, Chone Lama's personal name.

SUTRA (San.)   In the Tibetan tradition *sutra* generally refers to a scripture attributed to the historical BUDDHA Shakyamuni, and *tantra* to a scripture believed to have been taught by the Buddha in his esoteric form as VAJRADHARA. Sometimes the terms are used in a generic sense to refer to two distinct systems of thought and practice, the first roughly corresponding to general Buddhism and the latter to esoteric Buddhism (for example, "A Meditation on Impermanence" by Gungthang).

TANTRA (San.)   See SUTRA.

TASHI KHYIL   A famous GELUK monastery in AMDO founded by Jamyang Shepa (1648–1722) at the turn of the eighteenth century.

TEN DIRECTIONS   Four cardinal and four intermediate directions—east, west, north, south, and southeast, southwest, northwest, and northeast, plus the above and below points of the center.

TENPAI GYALTSEN   Name of one of the main teachers of Kalden Gyatso, one of the poets of our anthology.

THREE DISCIPLINES   The discipline of restraint, of engagement in virtuous acts, and of working for the benefit of other sentient beings. These three are also known as the three moralities.

THREE JEWELS   The BUDDHA (the enlightened teacher), the DHARMA (the way or the teaching), and the sangha (the spiritual community). In Buddhism, these three constitute true objects of refuge, for, by relying upon the three "jewels," an individual is said to gain freedom from suffering.

THREE KAYAS   See DHARMAKAYA.

THREE REALMS   According to Buddhist cosmology, unenlightened beings are said to revolve in a perpetual cycle of birth and death in three realms of existence: desire, form, and formlessness. The desire realm is characterized by an existence dictated by sensual experience; the form realm represents higher levels of consciousness; the formless realm constitutes the highest levels of being within an unenlightened state.

THREE SECRETS   The body, speech, and mind of a GURU or a highly realized spiritual person are often referred to as the three secrets, implying that the activities that arise from them are profound and beyond comprehension for an ordinary mind.

THREE SERVICES   Making offerings of gifts, rendering everyday help, and implementing one's teacher's instructions. Together, these three deeds constitute what are considered in Tibetan Buddhist teachings to be great offerings to one's spiritual teacher.

THREE STAGES OF BIRTH AND REBIRTH   Death, intermediate state, and rebirth. See also BARDO.

THREE TIMES   Past, present, and future.

THREE TYPES OF LAZINESS   Procrastination, lack of confidence, and indulgence in trivial activities. Although listed as three types of laziness, they are better understood as three aspects of laziness that together obstruct a person from engaging in any serious spiritual practice.

THREE VEHICLES   According to Tibetan Buddhism, all the teachings of the BUDDHA fall within the framework of what are called the three vehicles (or *yana* in Sanskrit). They are the Lesser Vehicle (Hinayana), the Great Vehicle (MAHAYANA), and the Diamond Vehicle (VAJRAYANA). The Lesser Vehicle teachings relate to the practices aimed primarily at the attainment of individual freedom from suffering and its underlying causes. Historically, these teachings are part of the Buddha's first public sermon at which the Buddhist principle of the four noble truths was presented. In contrast, the Great Vehicle presents a universal path wherein the fundamental spiritual goal and aspiration of the practitioner is the enlightenment of all beings. The key practices of the Great Vehicle are presented within the framework of the SIX PERFECTIONS. Often referred to by contemporary writers as "esoteric Buddhism," the Diamond Vehicle (Vajrayana) presents a sophisticated system of refining the fundamental Great Vehicle ideal of the union of method and wisdom. See also VAJRAYANA.

THREE VOWS Refers to three sets of vows an average Tibetan Buddhist practitioner observes. The first is "individually liberating vows" and pertains to the observance of an ethically disciplined way of life in the sense of conventional morality. The second relates to the practice of altruism and is known as the "BODHISATTVA vow," while the third set pertains to practices of esoteric Buddhism and is thus called the "tantric vows" (see SUTRA). The idea behind the observance of the three vows is that a practitioner's behavior must be firmly grounded in sound ethics; his or her outlook and attitude must reflect the altruistic concerns of a bodhisattva; and he or she must possess an inner life of spirituality that is rich in mystical experience.

TORMA (Tib.) A cake used for appeasing spirits. The sort envisaged by Drukpa Künlek in "Response to a Request for Teaching on Cause and Effect" is characteristically triangular and red in color.

TSANGPO RIVER Brahmaputra River, which flows from MOUNT KAILASH through Tibet into India.

TSARI MOUNTAIN A holy place located in central Tibet that is a popular site of pilgrimage for Tibetan Buddhists. Many of Shapkar's songs were written when visiting Tsari (for example, "A Song by a Yogi in Solitude").

TSONGKHAPA See "Biographies of the Poets."

TURQUOISE DRAGON In Tibetan mythological paintings, the thunder dragon is often depicted with a turquoise-colored mane.

TWENTY-FOUR POWER PLACES In the literature associated with CHAKRASAMVARA practice, twenty-four "power places" are identified, most of which are in the central and northern parts of India.

ULTIMATE TRUTH In Buddhist philosophy, the nature of reality is understood in terms of two truths, the relative and the ultimate. According to MADHYAMAKA philosophy, the perspective that all the poets of our anthology adopt, the ultimate nature of reality is said to be EMPTINESS. This is the nonsubstantiality of all things, including one's own identity and the world. It is insight into this ultimate truth that is said to be the key to enlightenment according to Madhyamaka thought.

VAIBHASHIKA (San.)   One of the four classical Indian Buddhist philosophical schools, Vaibhashika propounded a radical pluralism in that it accepted the notion of independently existing "atomic" factors called dharmas that are distinct and constitute both the material world and consciousness. It also accepted the substantial reality of time wherein both past and future are perceived to be as real as the present. A principal work of this Buddhist school is Vasubandhu's *Treasury of Knowledge*. Changkya's long poem "Recognizing My Mother" consoles the followers of Vaibhashika, suggesting that one need not subscribe to such radical pluralism in order to safeguard the reality of the external world.

VAJRA AND SPACE   In the language of esoteric Buddhism, *vajra* (literally "diamond," "scepter," or "adamantine") refers to the male organ and *space* to the female organ. Thus Chone Lama writes "the secret act of conjoining space and vajra" (in "A Dance of Unwavering Devotion").

VAJRADHARA (San.)   Literally meaning the "Holder of Vajra," Vajradhara is the BUDDHA Shakyamuni in his esoteric form according to the Tibetan tradition. He is the primordial Buddha, the sovereign over all Buddha-families, and the source of all important teachings of VAJRAYANA Buddhism. Because of this, it is quite customary in the Tibetan Buddhist tradition to refer to one's personal GURU as Vajradhara (as in "On the Death of Kyabje Trijhang Rinpoche" by Zemey Lobsang Palden).

VAJRAYANA (San.)   Literally meaning the "Diamond Vehicle," Vajrayana embodies the most profound teachings of the BUDDHA according to Tibetan Buddhism. A key feature of this system is the emphasis on nonduality as a fundamental perspective and the vision of final enlightenment as constituting the perfection of all aspects of the human psyche, especially the powerful emotions. In terms of method, Vajrayana teachings employ complex and colorful art and imagery pregnant with rich psychological symbolism as essential elements of meditative practices. At the heart of such meditations is a sophisticated system of visualization and identification of oneself with a meditation DEITY known as "Deity Yoga," and it is through formal empowerment ceremonies, such as the Kalachakra initiation performed by the Dalai Lama, that one is initiated into the practice. There are four classes within the Vajrayana system: (1) Performance Tantra, (2) Action Tantra, (3) Yoga Tantra, and (4) Highest Yoga Tantra.

VARAHI (San.)   The consort of Chakrasamvara. See also CHAKRASAMVARA.

VIEW   Tibetan Buddhist teachings speak of view, meditation, and action as constituting the three key elements of a spiritual practice. *View* refers to the cultivation and adoption of a correct outlook on life, while *meditation* suggests the importance of internalizing such an outlook. It is considered crucial that spiritual practitioners ensure that their view and meditation have a direct impact upon their behavior and action. In many of the poems, when the poets speak of the view, they are usually referring to a profound understanding of the view of EMPTINESS.

VIJNANAVADA (San.)   The "Mind Only" school of MAHAYANA Buddhism founded by Asanga (ca. fourth century) and his half brother Vasubandhu (ca. fourth century). It is sometimes referred to as Chittamatra ("Mind Only") or Yogachara ("Practice of Yoga"). According to the Tibetan tradition, there are four classical Indian Buddhist philosophical schools, namely VAIBHASHIKA, SAUTRANTIKA, Vijnanavada, and MADHYAMAKA. The central thesis of the Mind Only school was that our perception of external reality is false and that the ultimate nature of reality is the mind in its fundamental state. They propounded a theory of the nonduality of subject and object, whereby the object is subsumed within a basic substratum that is ultimately subjective. In "Recognizing My Mother," Changkya attributes the notion of "absence of duality" to the followers of this school.

VITAL DROPS   The idea of vital drops is an essential aspect of esoteric Buddhism and is related to concepts of CHANNELS and "energies." Though called drops, they are better understood as the refined essence of the regenerative fluids that are vital for the generation of blissful sexual experiences such as orgasm. The Tibetan word *thig-le* (literally "drops") carries the sense of a concentrated center of essential elements. Many of the visualizations in esoteric Buddhist meditation involve deliberate manipulation of these forces to induce profound levels of bliss and insight.

VOID, VOIDNESS   See EMPTINESS.

WATER-TIGER YEAR   The Tibetan calendar operates according to a cycle of sixty years, during which each of the twelve year signs is correlated to five elements: earth, iron, water, wood, and fire. The twelve year signs are rat, bull, tiger, hare, dragon, snake, horse, sheep, monkey, bird, dog, pig. The water-tiger year referred to by Chone Lama Rinpoche in "A Spontaneous Song Evoked by the Dream-Girl" is 1842.

WIND ENERGIES   The vital energies that are said to flow in the various CHANNELS in a human body according to esoteric Buddhist teachings. See also CHAKRAS.

YAMA (San.)   In both Buddhist and Hindu mythologies, Yama is the lord of death and is the sovereign of both the hell realms and the southern direction of the universe. (See "A Meditation on Impermanence" and "Ramblings of an Aged Man.") Often he is referred to simply as the lord of death (for example, in "*from* Tunes on the Absence of Elaborations" by Za Paltrül).

YOGA (San.)   The Tibetan equivalent of the term *naljor* has the connotation of fusing one's mind with the object of meditation. Thus in the Tibetan Buddhist context the term refers primarily to a meditative state of mind or a practice rather than to a system of physical exercise, as is the case with the anglicized usage of the word. For example, the Tibetan texts speak of "DEITY Yoga," "GURU Yoga," the "yoga of GENERATION STAGE," the "yoga of COMPLETION STAGE," and so on. See also YOGI and YOGIN.

YOGI   An anglicized spelling of YOGIN.

YOGIN (San.)   A meditator, a wandering mystic, or an adept (for example, in "At the Feet of the Lord of Dance" by Karma Trinley). The term is derived from *yoga*, which means "union," or "nonduality," signifying a transcendental state of mind whereby the practitioner has attained a deepened state of meditative consciousness.

YOGINI (San.)   A female YOGIN, a meditator or a mystic. Sometimes *yogini* is also used to refer to a dakini. See also DAKINIS.

ZOKCHEN (Tib.)   According to the NYINGMA classification of the Buddhist systems of thought and practice, Zokchen—literally "Great Perfection"—is said to be the highest. The defining feature of this practice is the pervasive emphasis it places on the allowing of the natural expression of what is called

RIKPA, intrinsic awareness. There is an understanding that the entire expanse of reality is nothing but different modalities of an underlying basic truth, that is, a pristine awareness. "An Adamantine Song on Purposeless Pursuits" and "An Adamantine Song on the Ever-Present" by Longchen Rabjampa articulate in some detail the various dimensions of the rikpa awareness.

ZOKPA CHENPO (Tib.)   The same as ZOKCHEN, which is the abbreviation of Zokpa Chenpo.

Biographies of the Poets

All cross-references appear in small capitals.

CHANGKYA RÖLPAI DORJE (1717–1786)

Changkya Rölpai Dorje was born to an ethnic Mongolian family in the Tsong-kha region of Amdo near the northeastern border of Tibet and China in 1717. At the age of four, the young boy was recognized as the reincarnation of Changkya Lobsang Chöden and invited by the Chinese emperor Yun Ting to enter the monastery of his predecessor Changkya Rinpoche in China. He took his first precepts at the age of seven. By eighteen, Changkya had not only become learned in many subjects of Buddhist studies but had also mastered the Chinese, Manchurian, and Mongolian languages. At the age of nineteen he traveled to central Tibet and met the seventh Dalai Lama, KELSANG GYATSO. While in central Tibet, Changkya took his novitiate vows from Panchen Lobsang Yeshe (1663–1737). However, Changkya's stay in central Tibet abruptly came to an end when he had to return to Peking following the death of the emperor Yun Ting. At the age of twenty-five, in his capacity as chief editor, Changkya Rölpai Dorje supervised the translation of the entire *Tangyur* (the commentarial translations of the Tibetan canon) from Tibetan into Mongolian. He revisited his birthplace at the age of thirty-three and taught extensively at Kumbum monastery.

Starting at the age of fifty-one, Changkya spent four months each summer at his newly built retreat at Wu Tai Shan, the Five Peaks Mountain associated with Manjushri in Shanxi province in China. When he was fifty-five Changkya was once again called upon, because of his scholarly and linguistic skills, to help translate the entire Tibetan canon, this time into Manchurian. Changkya's writings include, in addition to various experiential songs such as the one included in this volume, the highly acclaimed *Philosophical Tenets*, which later became an authoritative source for Buddhist philosophical studies. He died in 1786 at his much-loved retreat at Wu Tai Shan.

Chone Lama Lodrö Gyatso (b. 1816)

Lodrö Gyatso, popularly known as Chone Lama Rinpoche, was born in the Amdo province of northeastern Tibet in 1816. Despite his fame, there is scant information concerning his life. Based on the little that is known, at the age of nine the young Lodrö Gyatso entered Tashi Khyil monastery, where he studied for several years before departing for central Tibet to pursue further studies at Drepung monastery. It seems that after the completion of his training at Drepung, Lodrö Gyatso returned to his native Amdo. There he succeeded to the abbotship of several monasteries, including the famous Labrang Tashi Khyil. Judging by his writings, Lodrö Gyatso appears to have spent a significant part of his life in solitary meditation. His works include a rich collection of experiential songs and also the highly acclaimed verse commentary on a short text by TSONGKHAPA known as *In Praise of Dependent Origination*.

Drakpa Gyaltsen (1147–1216)

Drakpa Gyaltsen was the younger brother of Jetsun Sönam Tsemo and the son of one of the great Sakya founding fathers, Sachen Kunga Nyingpo. It is said that from the time he learned to speak, Drakpa always expressed deep yearning for the life of a wandering meditator. He took his first precepts at the age of eight and is said to have begun teaching when he was ten. After the death of his father and brother, Drakpa Gyaltsen assumed the responsibilities of the main master at Sakya monastery, when he was only thirteen. He was to remain in this position until he was seventy. His learning in all fields of Buddhist thought and practice, and especially in the vast transmission of the contemplative traditions, became highly respected. Drakpa Gyaltsen was especially noted for his great dedication to his meditative practice; such was his skillfulness and mastery of meditation that it is said that he was able to turn every event of life into a religious experience. Drakpa Gyaltsen wrote many songs that record his personal religious and meditative experiences. His students include the famous Sakya Pandita Kunga Gyaltsen. Drakpa Gyaltsen died in 1216.

Drukpa Künlek (1455–1570)

Born the youngest of seven brothers, Drukpa Künlek lost his father at an early age. He was brought up under the charge of his aunt, who gave him as an attendant to the head of the Rinpung family in Tsang province. After six turbulent years with the Rinpung family while its power was being challenged from various corners, Drukpa Künlek left on a religious quest. He embarked upon a journey, traveling from place to place, taking teachings, meditating, and reflecting on the meaning of the scriptures. Drukpa Künlek spent much of his time in Bhutan, Taklung, and Kongpo, and visited various places in Tibet. Many of his personal experiences during these travels—including the deepening of his meditative realization—are recorded in his autobiographical songs of experience, from which one poem is included in the present volume.

Drukpa Künlek's somewhat iconoclastic songs are revolutionary within the genre of Tibetan religious writing. In his verses Drukpa Künlek makes mockery of academic scholasticism, self-righteous morality, ritual formalism, the abuse of authority by those in power, the exploitation of the superstitious, and the corruption of religious institutions. These songs endeared Drukpa Künlek to the general public so much that, together with Aku Tönpa (the legendary rascal of Tibet), he became popularly known as a divine madman, or a jester saint. To this day his songs are sung and his stories are passed on from generation to generation. According to his biography, Drukpa Künlek died in 1570, at the age of 115, at his son's monastery in Tölung.

Gungthang Tenpai Drönme (1762–1822)

Gungthang Tenpai Drönme, popularly known as Gungthang Jampel-yang, was born in Dzoge in the Amdo province of northeastern Tibet. At the age of seven he was recognized by Jamyang Shepa Könchok Jigme Wangpo as the reincarnation of Trichen Gendün Phüntsok and invited to enter Tashi Khyil monastery. He received his novitiate vows from Könchok Jigme Wangpo, who also gave him the personal name Könchok Tenpai Drönme. In 1778, Gungthang entered the Gomang college of Drepung monastery in Lhasa. By the age of twenty-one, when he sat for his formal examination, Gungthang's scholarship was widely recognized in central Tibet. While in central Tibet, he wrote a number of works on various aspects of Buddhist philosophical studies.

At twenty-four Gungthang returned to Tashi Khyil in Amdo, where in 1791 he succeeded to the abbotship of the monastery. He taught extensively in Amdo while at the same time engaging in meditative practices and writing. His works include, in addition to numerous pieces on philosophy, a collection of various poems. Gungthang was a master ironist who wrote in Tibetan with great ease and fluency. The famous Palmang Könchok Gyaltsen was among Gungthang's students. Gungthang died in 1822.

KALDEN GYATSO (1607–1677)

Kalden Gyatso (known also as Shar Kalden Gyatso or Rongpo Kalden Gyatso) was born in Gyalthang in Amdo province, in northeastern Tibet. From the age of four he was brought up and educated by his half brother, the meditator Chöpa Rinpoche, who later gave him the novitiate vows. At the age of eleven Kalden Gyatso accompanied his brother to central Tibet. He entered the Jhangtse college of Ganden monastery, where he studied for ten years and became a scholar of great reputation. He took full ordination from Panchen Lobsang Chögyen at the age of twenty. Following his ordination, Kalden Gyatso returned to Amdo, where he established several retreat places and the monastery of Thösam Nampar Gyalwe Ling. When he reached the age of thirty, Kalden Gyatso began to lead the life of a wandering monk, traveling place to place, often on pilgrimage, and meditating in solitude. He acquired the name of *drupchen*, the great meditator.

Kalden Gyatso met the fifth Dalai Lama in 1652 when the latter was on his way to China. Along with the great Jamyang Shepa Ngagwang Tsöndru, Kalden Gyatso was formally recognized as having made the greatest contributions toward the perpetuation of the teachings of the Buddha in Amdo province. Kalden Gyatso was especially known for his profound compassion and deep spiritual realization. His emphasis on the practice-orientated religious life was such that a new order of mendicants known as *ritröpa* ("those of the wilderness") emerged. Some of the songs by Kalden Gyatso included in the present volume were written by the author during his travels. Kalden Gyatso died at the retreat of Tashi Khyil in Amdo in 1677.

KARMA TRINLEY (1456–1539)

Following his ordination into the monastic life at the age of seventeen, Karma Trinley entered formal education in various topics of Buddhist studies, including the practice lineages of the Kagyü school of Tibetan Buddhism. He studied with masters of the Kadam school, the Sakya school, and of course his own Kagyü tradition, especially Chödrak Gyatso, the fourth hierarch of the Shamar lineage. Around the age of thirty Karma Trinley began to experience powerful visions of meditation deities, especially during his pilgrimage to the holy mountain of Tsari. He is said to have had an encounter with the protector spirit Shingkyong there, which was to have a powerful impact upon his life. Later Karma Trinley became a highly realized yogin of the mystical feminine teachings of Vajrayogini. Karma Trinley became one of the main tutors to the young Mikyö Dorje, the eighth Karmapa. He founded Lekshe Ling monastery, which later became one of the main seats of learning in the Karma Kagyü lineage of Tibetan Buddhism. Karma Trinley spent much of the latter part of his life in meditative retreat, often writing about his personal experiences.

KELSANG GYATSO, SEVENTH DALAI LAMA (1708–1757)

Kelsang Gyatso was born in Lithang in Kham province in the eastern part of Tibet. His birth was accompanied by auspicious signs, including the utterance of certain prophesies by a wandering mystic who gave the boy the name Kelsang Gyatso. It is said that at the early age of five, Kelsang Gyatso had a mysterious experience in which TSONGKHAPA exhorted him to go to central Tibet. The word of his prodigious gift for extempore verse composition soon spread, attracting people who came to receive teachings from the young boy. In 1716, Kelsang Gyatso left Lithang and was received by many monasteries in Kham on his way to Lhasa. At the birthplace of Tsongkhapa he was installed on the throne of the third Dalai Lama, Sönam Gyatso, and delivered a sermon to a congregation of several thousand devotees.

Kelsang Gyatso took his first precepts at the age of nine at Kumbum monastery. He was installed at the Potala palace when he reached the age of thirteen. There he took his novitiate vows from Panchen Lobsang Yeshe (1663–1737), and studied the classical Buddhist texts with many great scholars of his time. He received full ordination in 1735 from the Panchen Lama in the presence of the famous statue of Buddha Shakyamuni inside the central temple of Lhasa. Around this time, because of the uncertain political climate in central Tibet, Kelsang Gyatso left for Kham. Throughout his long journey, he visited many towns and monasteries and gave teachings to his devotees. In 1751 he assumed temporal power as the seventh Dalai Lama and immediately set in motion the creation of the first Tibetan *kashak* (cabinet office) to ensure a greater degree of consensus in the decision-making procedure. Though ostensibly a ruler of a country, in his own private life Kelsang Gyatso remained first and foremost a scholar and a committed religious practitioner. He wrote extensively on many aspects of Buddhist theory and practice, and also numerous songs of spiritual experience. The pieces included in this volume are some of the best-loved poems of the seventh Dalai Lama. His students include Panchen Palden Yeshe, CHANGKYA RÖLPAI DORJE (who wrote the official biography of the seventh Dalai Lama), and Demo Gelek Gyatso. He died in 1757 at the Potala palace.

LONGCHEN RABJAMPA (1308–1363)

Longchen Rabjampa (also known as Longchen Drimey Öser) was born in Yoru in Tsang province, in central Tibet. By the age of five the young boy had begun to receive teachings on various Nyingma lineages from his father, who also taught him medicine and astrology. When he was twelve, Longchenpa received his novitiate vows, was given the name Tsultrim Lodrö, and started receiving many important Vajrayana instructions. At the age of nineteen the young Longchenpa entered the monastery of Sangphu—a major seat of philosophical learning in central Tibet—where he studied many of the Indian Buddhist classical texts on logic and epistemology, Middle Way philosophy, and many other subjects. It was in recognition of his great learning that the name Rabjampa ("one who is in abundance") was given to him. Later Longchenpa received many important contemplative teachings from the third Karmapa, RANGJUNG DORJE; he also received various lineages of the Sakya school, in particular the teachings of the Lamdre ("path and fruition") tradition.

Interestingly, it is said that at Sangphu monastery Longchenpa felt deeply hurt by the behavior of some of the monks from Kham, in eastern Tibet. This led the young Longchenpa to wish to leave the monastery for a life of solitary practice. Eventually he was persuaded by many of his students and peers to stay. They suggested that Longchenpa write on a paper what he felt were the misdemeanors of the Khampa monks, a piece that was later pasted on a wall in the debating courtyard. Soon after, Longchenpa did embark on a journey to travel as a wandering mendicant.

During one such journey, Longchenpa is said to have had a profound mystical experience, which took the form of hearing melodious music. This was to be an early indication of the maturing of his destiny, which would lead him to encounter the profound teachings of the Zokchen practice. It was only at the age of twenty-nine that Longchenpa finally met his guru, Rigdzin Kumaraja, who was to initiate him into the rich traditions of the Zokchen meditative tradition. Longchenpa's practice of Zokchen would gradually lead him into a series of mystical communions with Dorje Yudrönma (a protectress), which culminated in the revelation of the Indian master Vimalamitra's secret writings on the essential practices of Zokchen. Longchenpa thus became the authoritative medium and interpreter of this important Buddhist mystical tradition, which later became known as Vima Nyingthik ("the heart drop of Vimalamitra"). Longchenpa's works on Zokchen—especially his trilogy called *Kindly Bent to Ease Us*, the seven *Treasures*, and his commentary on the seminal work *Guhyagarbha*—remain, to this day, the authoritative source on the key doctrines of the Zokchen teachings of the Nyingma school of Tibetan Buddhism.

MACHIK LABDRÖN (1055–1143)

Machik Labdrön is probably the most revered woman mystic in Tibet. She was born in a place called Kheugang in Tibet. She received her ordination as a nun at an early age and became an expert reader of the scriptures. Once, while reading the *Perfection of Wisdom* scriptures, Machik Labdrön experienced a profound insight into the emptiness of all phenomena. Around this time she also came into contact with the mystic Pha Dampa Sangye; together they later became known as the founders of the Chöd ("cutting off") practice tradition. Later she met her future husband, Thöpa Ba-re, with whom Machik went to Kongpo. It is said that one of the reasons she left for Kongpo was the constant criticism made by people calling her names such as "the nun who has violated her vows." With her husband she had two daughters and three sons.

Later Machik returned to her nun's life, traveling from place to place. During one of these travels, Machik attended an empowerment ceremony in Kham, conducted by Kyo Sönam Lama. It is said that she attained profound realizations while she was in the middle of the ceremony, at which point she got up to leave. This was scandalous for the congregation, but the initiator lama saw what had actually occurred. He told the rest of the congregation that while all of them received empowerment verbally, only Machik had truly experienced it. A characteristic of her Chöd practice was to sing songs of profound mystical experience while playing a large drum held in her right hand. Such singing often occurred at night at places that challenged the very being of one's person, such as charnel grounds or haunted ruins. The piece included in this volume is a typical example of such songs. Her lineage of

Chöd practice spread all over Tibet and exerted influence on all established traditions of Tibetan Buddhism.

MILAREPA (1040–1123)

Milarepa is one of the most loved religious figures in Tibetan history and also the most popular of all religious mystics. Milarepa's life as a poet, saint, meditator, and mendicant captured the imagination of the Tibetan people. Such was the influence of his legend that his life became the standard by which the dedication and tenacity of one's meditative practice is judged. Born into a somewhat humble background, Milarepa (then known as Thöpaga) suffered the tragedy of his father's death when he was in his early teens. His family, including his mother and younger sister, then came under the care of some despotic relatives who took charge of Milarepa's ancestral properties. He and his family were treated as hired servants in the new family and were often cruelly mistreated. This angered Milarepa's mother so much that, it is said, she sent the young boy to train in black magic to take revenge against their oppressors. Legend has it that a thunder- and hailstorm broke out that destroyed the house of the relatives when there was a wedding ceremony taking place and killed some members of the family. This incident led the young Milarepa to such grief and remorse that he vowed to atone for his sins.

In his quest for genuine spiritual guidance, Milarepa met the great translator Marpa Lotsawa, who became his master. From Marpa, Milarepa received all the profound lineages of the mystical teachings that Marpa himself had received from the Indian mystic Naropa. Milarepa put this teaching into single-pointed practice in his lifestyle as a wandering mystic. The latter part of Milarepa's life represents a triumph of good over evil and is a testimony to the fruits of hardship and endeavor in one's spiritual quest. The story of Milarepa's unwavering devotion to his master, Marpa, is seen by subsequent Tibetan practitioners as the supreme example of an ideal guru-disciple relationship as exhorted in the Buddhist scriptures. Many of Milarepa's profound mystical experiences are encapsulated in the *Hundred Thousand Songs of Milarepa*, which were compiled by Tsang Nyön Heruka in the sixteenth century. Milarepa's two closest disciples were Rechungpa (1084–1161) and Gampopa (1079–1153), the latter being the author of the famous *Jewel Ornament of Liberation*. Together with his teacher, Marpa Lotsawa, and his disciple Gampopa, Milarepa is considered to be a founder of the Kagyü school of Tibetan Buddhism. Milarepa died in 1123.

Natsok Rangdröl (b. 1608)

Natsok Rangdröl is believed to be a reincarnation of the famous Nyingma master and treasure-text revealer Ratna Lingpa (1403–1478). He studied at the feet of many great Tibetan masters of all schools of Tibetan Buddhism; in particular Natsok Rangdröl studied the Zokchen teachings of Longchen Rabjampa with Kunga Gyaltsen and Master Mati Dhvaja. Following a long period of study, Natsok Rangdröl spent many years in intensive meditation at various retreats, such as Chim Phu Sheldrak in central Tibet. In addition to gaining deep insight into the profound teachings of Zokchen, Natsok Rangdröl is also said to have experienced visions of meditation deities. Subsequent to his mystical experience, Natsok Rangdröl traveled extensively in various parts of central and southern Tibet engaging in numerous teaching and meditation practices.

Rangjung Dorje, third Karmapa (1284–1339)

Rangjung Dorje began to have mystical experiences from a very early age. The two events that are believed to have triggered his visions were the young boy's pilgrimage to Dingri, the holy site of the mystic Pha Dampa Sangye, at the age of three, and his visit to the shrine of Avalokiteshvara (the Buddha of compassion) in Kyirong, western Tibet. At the age of five Rangjung Dorje was recognized by the Tibetan master Drupchen Ogyen as the third reincarnation of Karmapa. It is said that one day Drupchen Ogyen told his disciples that his teacher would be visiting him the next day, and he had a high throne decorated and ready. It was actually the young boy of five who arrived with his parents to receive blessings from the master. Upon their arrival, the boy instantly climbed upon the throne. He is reported to have said, "Although I am the lama, as I have to rely on you, now I should get off the throne." Thus began a fruitful guru-disciple relationship between the young boy and Drupchen Ogyen. Rangjung continued to have mystical experiences, and gradually his fame began to spread.

Rangjung Dorje took full ordination when he was eighteen and embarked upon a full-fledged formal religious education at Tsurphu monastery, the seat of the Karmapas. He traveled across central and western Tibet, and also to Kham in eastern Tibet. The poems by Rangjung Dorje included in this collection were written during a pilgrimage to Tsari, a popular holy site in the southern part of Tibet associated with the mystical lineages of Heruka. In

1331 Rangjung Dorje visited Mongolia, and in 1334 he went on a pilgrimage to Wu Tai Shan, the Five Peaks Mountain associated with Manjushri (the Buddha of wisdom) in northern China. During his travels Rangjung Dorje taught extensively and established many retreats and monasteries all across Tibet. He also mediated in many long-standing familial disputes in Kham. Rangjung Dorje died in 1339 in China.

SHAPKAR TSOGDRUK RANGDRÖL (1781–1851)

Shapkar was born in the village of Showong Nyengya in the Amdo province of northeastern Tibet. At the age of eight he entered the local monastery, Ngagmang Chothok, where he studied until the age of ten. Later the young Shapkar met the masters Jamyang Gyatso and Ogyen Trinley, from whom he received many teachings. When he was twenty-one, Shapkar took the full ordination and became a monk. Over the next six years, Shapkar studied extensively with the learned scholar Ngawang Dargye and achieved a high level of scholarship. It was in 1806 that Shapkar began his thirty-year journey as a wandering mystic, traveling to various sites of pilgrimage such as Tsari in the south and Mount Kailash in the west, as well as Machen, Tsonying, and Drakar Trelzong in the eastern and northeastern parts of Tibet. Many of Shapkar's personal experiences and thoughts during this period are recorded in a lengthy set of autobiographical poems, *The Life of Shapkar*. Poems included in this volume are taken from this source. Shapkar's life as a wandering poet became so well known that people began to call him the second MILAREPA. He died in 1851 at his own birthplace.

TSANGPA GYARE (1161–1211)

Tsangpa Gyare was born in the Nyangtö region of eastern Tibet as the youngest of seven children. It is said that Tsangpa Gyare's father did not care much about the new child. Thus his mother felt that he would be better looked after if she were to give him to a family that had no children of their own, which is what she did. The death of his mother when he was eight left a strong impression on the young Tsangpa Gyare. At the age of thirteen he began formal religious training and studies with a number of great masters of his time, in particular the great Kagyü master Jetsün Lingchen Repa. So, by the age of twenty-two, Tsangpa Gyare had already established himself as a noted scholar. However, it was not until he took the transmissions of the mystical teachings of Mahamudra and Zokchen that he found his true personal path. He became a well-known master of the Drukpa Kagyü lineage of the Tibetan Buddhist contemplative traditions.

The single-pointedness of his dedication to meditative practice and the profundity of his experience were such that people began to compare him to the great poet-saint MILAREPA. Despite his deep mystical realizations, Tsangpa Gyare is said to have striven for a long time to seek an effective practice for perfecting the great bodhisattva ideal of universal compassion. As part of this quest, Tsangpa Gyare adopted the life of a celibate monk at the age of thirty-three. After his ordination, Tsangpa Gyare spent the rest of his life in the altruistic pursuit of the fulfillment of the principles of compassion. He traveled extensively in the regions of Tsang, many nomadic areas, and Bhutan, teaching, mediating in disputes, establishing centers of learning. It is said that in his teachings to the disciples, Tsangpa Gyare emphasized three principal points: (1) the need to develop a deep sense of revulsion to the bondage of mundane existence, (2) the need to adopt a life of single-pointed religious practice, and finally, (3) the need always to ground the first two principles on an unshakable respect and reverence for one's spiritual teacher. Tsangpa Gyare died in 1211.

TSONGKHAPA (1357–1419)

Tsongkhapa was born in the Tsongkha region of Amdo province in the northeastern part of Tibet. His birth was accompanied by a number of auspicious signs, including the dreams of Master Döndup Rinchen (b. 1309), which eventually led to his taking charge of the early education of the boy. At the age of three the young Tsongkhapa took his first precepts from the third Karmapa, RANGJUNG DORJE, and was given the name Kunga Nyingpo. From the age of seven, Kunga Nyingpo began to receive from Döndup Rinchen a series of initiations into the mystical teachings of Vajrayana Buddhism. He also received his novitiate vows and entered the monastic order; from then onward he became known as Lobsang Drakpa, the name he retained throughout his life. At sixteen Tsongkhapa left for central Tibet, where he studied at a number of learning centers, such as Sakya, Dewachen, Narthang, and Tsethang. His teachers include, in addition to Döndup Rinchen, the Sakya master Redawa Shönu Lodrö (1349–1412), Lama Umapa, and Drupchen Namkha Gyaltsen (1326–1401). By the time he took his full ordination at nineteen,

Tsongkhapa was already widely recognized as a great scholar. While continuing to deepen his own understanding of the Buddhist teachings and aspiring for deeper philosophical insights, he began to teach and write extensively.

It was, however, Tsongkhapa's encounter with Lama Umapa in 1370 that was to lead to his true destiny. Umapa was a mystic from Kham who was believed to commune with Manjushri (the Buddha of wisdom); he became a medium between Tsongkhapa and Manjushri, who engaged in a series of discourses. On the advice of Manjushri, Tsongkhapa spent a few years in solitary practice, taking with him only a handful of his closest disciples. This retreat was to culminate eventually in Tsongkhapa's own direct mystical communion with Manjushri, who is believed to have revealed the essence of the Middle Way philosophy of emptiness and the key teachings of the highest yoga practices of Vajrayana Buddhism. In the aftermath of this experience, Tsongkhapa embarked on a mission of disseminating his profound insights, mainly through writing and extensive teaching. His works written after the age of forty or forty-one are considered to represent Tsongkhapa's "mature" standpoint.

In 1409 Tsongkhapa founded Ganden monastery, which soon became an important center of learning in central Tibet. This was followed by the founding of Drepung in 1416 by Jamyang Chöje Tashi Palden, and Sera in 1419 by Jamchen Chöje Shakya Shenyen. Together they became the "great centers of learning" of the Geluk school of Tibetan Buddhism. Tsongkhapa's great contribution lies in his revitalization of the Middle Way philosophy, a systematization of the synthesis of the scholastic and mystical dimensions of Tibetan Buddhism, and not least, the restoration of monasticism in Tibet. Tsongkhapa himself summed up his life in the following manner:

> At the beginning, I engaged in vast learning,
> In the middle, I perceived all teachings as instructions,
> Finally, I strove in meditative practice day and night.

Tsongkhapa died at Ganden in 1419.

ZA PALTRÜL (1808–1887)

Za Paltrül, whose full name is Paltrul Jigme Chökyi Wangpo, was born in the valley of Dzachu in the northern part of Tibet. From an early age he was recognized as the reincarnation of Palge Samten Phuntsok. Za Paltrül spent most of his adult life as a meditator, often in solitude. He wrote poems about his experience, both celebrating, and at times lamenting the lack of progress in, his practice. His songs reflect a mind of a true meditator whose single-pointed quest for enlightenment shines with brilliance and a rare personal warmth. Included in the present volume are some of his finest verses, which never fail to evoke a spiritual dimension. Of all his works, perhaps the most highly acclaimed is *The Words of My Perfect Teacher*, a meditation manual for a step-by-step approach to the path of enlightenment. This text became the classic introduction to the Buddhist path within the Nyingma school of Tibetan Buddhism. Za Paltrül Rinpoche died in 1887.

ZEMEY LOBSANG PALDEN (1927–1996)

Zemey Lobsang Palden, one of the greatest Tibetan poets of the twentieth century, was born in Yangten, Kham, in the eastern part of Tibet. Following his recognition, at the age of three, as the reincarnation of the third Zemey Rinpoche, he began his training as the young reincarnate lama. Zemey Rinpoche received his novitiate precepts at the age of seven, and in 1937, when he was ten, the young Zemey entered Shartse college of Ganden monastery in central Tibet. There he studied for ten years and in 1948 obtained the Lharam Geshe degree, the traditional Tibetan equivalent of a doctorate in divinity. He then joined Gyutö college to pursue higher studies in Vajrayana Buddhism, and completed his formal education at the age of twenty-six. Zemey Rinpoche's scholarly reputation became established when, at twenty-eight, he published a lengthy philosophical critique of Gendun Chöphel's treatise on the Middle Way philosophy. From an early age, Zemey Rinpoche was groomed by the great Trijhang Rinpoche, the junior tutor to the Dalai Lama, to be the custodian of many important lineages of the contemplative practices of the Geluk tradition of Tibetan Buddhism.

Toward the end of the 1950s and especially in the period of exile after 1959, Zemey Rinpoche played a central role in the modernization of the Tibetan educational system. He served as a senior teacher at the first modern school to be established in Lhasa, and later accompanied His Holiness the Dalai Lama during his travels to India and China in 1957 and 1958, respectively. In exile in India, Zemey Rinpoche continued to work in education, first by writing the first Tibetan language textbooks and then by training the first teachers to be deputed to the various Tibetan schools in India and Nepal.

In 1974 he retired from active public service to lead a contemplative life at his retreat near Mysore, south India. Four years later he moved his residence to the reestablished monastic university of Ganden in Mundgod, south India, where he taught, wrote, and meditated—the pursuits he loved most. Included in this volume are some of the experiential songs that he wrote after his retirement. Zemey Rinpoche died in March 1996 at his residence at Tashi Gephel House at Ganden in south India.

Bibliography of Tibetan Works

Changkya Rölpai Dorje. *lTa mgur ama ngos 'dzin.* Xylograph reprint. Mundgod, India: Drepung Gomang, n.d.

Chone Lama Rinpoche. *The Collected Works of Chone Lama Rinpoche.* Dharamsala, India: Library of Tibetan Works and Archives, 1976.

Drakpa Gyaltsen. "The Collected Works of rJe btsun Grags pa rGyal mtshan" in *Collected Works of the Masters of the Sakya Sect.* Vol. 4. Tokyo: Toyo Bunko, 1968.

Drukpa Künlek. *'Gro-ba 'i mGon-po Kun-dga 'Legs-pa'i rnam thar mon spa gro sogs kyi mdzad spyod.* Dharamsala, India: Tibetan Cultural Printing Press, 1981.

Gungthang Tenpai Drönme (1). *The Collected Works of Gun-than dKon-mchog bsTan-pa'i sGron-me.* Vol. 4. New Delhi: Ngawang Gelek Demo, 1972.

Gungthang Tenpai Drönme (2). *The Collected Works of Gun-than dKon-mchog bsTan-pa'i sGron-me.* Vol. 9. New Delhi: Ngawang Gelek Demo, 1979.

Kalden Gyatso. *Grub dbang sKal-ldan rGya-mtsho'i mgur 'bum.* Varanasi, India: Rigjung Dongkhyer Publications, 1994.

Karma Trinley. *The Songs of Esoteric Practice (mgur) and Replies to Doctrinal Questions* (dris lan). New Delhi: 1975.

Kelsang Gyatso, seventh Dalai Lama. *The Collected Works (gsung 'bum) of the Seventh Dalai Lama blo bzang bskal bzang rgya mtsho.* Vol. 1. New Delhi: Dodrup Sangye, 1995.

Longchen Rabjampa. *The Collected Works of Klon-chen-pa Dri-med 'Od-zer.* Vol. 2. New Delhi: Sangye Dorje, 1973.

Machik Labdrön. In *gDams ngag mdzod.* Edited by Kong-sprul Yon-tan rGya-mtsho. Vol. 4. New Delhi: 1971.

Milarepa. *rNal 'byor gyi dbang phyug Mi-la Ras-pa'i rnam mgur.* Dharamsala, India: Tibetan Cultural Printing Press, 1990.

Natsok Rangdröl. *Collected Works of rTse-le sNa-tshogs Ran-grol.* Vol. 1. New Delhi: Sangye Dorje, 1974.

Rangjung Dorje, third Karmapa. *Rang-byung rDo-rje'i mGur-rnam.* Thimphu, Bhutan: 1983.

Shapkar Tsogdruk Rangdröl. *Gangs ljongs mkhas dbang rim byon gyi rtsom yig gser gyi sbram bu.* Vol. 3. Xining, China: Qingai Minorities Press, 1988.

Tsangpa Gyare. *The Collected Songs of gTsang-pa rGya-ras.* Darjeeling, India: Kagyud Sungrab Nyamso Khang, 1972.

Tsongkhapa. *rJe Tsong kha pa chen po'i bka' 'bum thor bu.* Xining, China: Qingai Minorities Press, 1987.

Za Paltrül. *The Collected Works of dPal sprul 'Jigs med Chos kyi dBang po.* Vol. 6. Gangtok, India: Sönam Kazi, 1971.

Zemey Lobsang Palden. *Collected Works of Kyabje Zemey Rinpoche.* Compiled and edited by Geshe Thupten Jinpa. Vol. 5. Xylograph format, Mundgod, India: Tashi Gephel House, 1997.

Sources for the Poems

The following is a list of the page references from the original Tibetan sources of the poems collected here. For a complete reference, see the bibliography.

EVOCATIONS OF LIFE'S TRANSIENCE

from "Tunes on the Absence of Elaborations," Za Paltrül Rinpoche, pp. 399–400.

"A Meditation on Impermanence," Gungthang Tenpai Drönme (1), pp. 118–121.

"Movements of Dancing Lightning," Chone Lama Rinpoche, pp. 131–134.

"A Word-Brush Drawing . . . ," Chone Lama Rinpoche, pp. 144–147.

"Inspire Me to Remember Death," Kelsang Gyatso, seventh Dalai Lama, pp. 421–424.

"Ramblings of an Aged Man," Gungthang Tenpai Drönme (2), pp. 283–291.

YEARNING FOR SOLITUDE

"The Red Rocky Mountain," Milarepa, p. 200.

"The Joys of the Solitary Hills," Kalden Gyatso, pp. 123–124.

"A Song by a Yogi in Solitude," Shapkar Tsogdruk Rangdröl, pp. 1539–41.

"Longing for the Mountains of Solitude," Za Paltrül Rinpoche, p. 412.

CALLING THE GURU FROM AFAR

"A Beggar and His Guru," Milarepa, p. 199.

"May I See My Guru Again and Again," Natsok Rangdröl, pp. 174–176.

"A Song of Desolation," Kalden Gyatso, p. 91.

"On the Death of Kyabje Trijhang Rinpoche," Zemey Lobsang Palden, pp. 100–103.

ECHOES OF EMPTINESS

"Reflections on Emptiness," Tsongkhapa, p. 218.

"In Praise of the Vision . . . ," Kelsang Gyatso, seventh Dalai Lama, pp. 415–416.

"Ramblings of a Drunken Bee," Chone Lama Rinpoche, pp. 55–58.

"A Response to a Logician," Milarepa, pp. 554–555.

"A Spontaneous Song Evoked by the Dream-Girl," Chone Lama Rinpoche, pp. 66–67.

"A Sky with a Center and Borders!" Longchen Rabjampa, pp. 378–381.

"Melodies of an Echo," Chone Lama Rinpoche, pp. 79–80.

"The Love Dance of Emptiness and Appearance," Chone Lama Rinpoche, pp. 105–106.

"Awake from the Slumber of Ignorance!" Kelsang Gyatso, seventh Dalai Lama, pp. 417–420.

"Recognizing My Mother," Changkya Rölpai Dorje, xylograph reprint. See bibliography.

Steps on the Path to Awakening

"An Experiential Tune on Eight Dream Practices," Drakpa Gyaltsen, p. 348.

"Lines of Self-Encouragement . . . ," Rangjung Dorje, third Karmapa, pp. 51–52.

"Wielding a Club in the Darkness," Tsangpa Gyare, pp. 222–224.

"A Song of Self-Encouragement . . . ," Chone Lama Rinpoche, pp. 187–188.

"Laying the Ground for Forbearance," Rangjung Dorje, third Karmapa, pp. 49–50.

"On How to Engage in a Meditative Path," Drakpa Gyaltsen, p. 349.

"A Prayer for the Flourishing of Virtues," Tsongkhapa, pp. 421–424.

Visions of Mystic Consciousness

"A Taste of Meditation," Tsangpa Gyare, pp. 219–220.

"The Dakinis' Feast," Natsok Rangdröl, pp. 168–169.

"An Adamantine Song on Purposeless Pursuits," Longchen Rabjampa, pp. 383–386.

"A Dance of Unwavering Devotion," Chone Lama Rinpoche, pp. 308–310.

"A Song on the View of Voidness," Karma Trinley, pp. 8–10.

"On How to Apply the Antidotes," Drakpa Gyaltsen, p. 348.

"Cutting the Rope of Conceit," Machik Labdrön, pp. 459–460.

"A Feast Song in Lhasa," Rangjung Dorje, third Karmapa, pp. 34–37.

"Hail to Manjushri!" Rangjung Dorje, third Karmapa, p. 46.

"A Vajra Song . . . ," Chone Lama Rinpoche, pp. 184–186.

"Little Tiger," Kelsang Gyatso, seventh Dalai Lama, pp. 476–478.

"An Adamantine Song on the Ever-Present," Longchen Rabjampa, pp. 377–378.

"On the Inner Practice of Secret Mantra," Drakpa Gyaltsen, p. 349.

"At the Feet of the Lord of Dance," Karma Trinley, pp. 15–16.

"In Response to a Request . . . ," Drukpa Künlek, pp. 58–61.

"Experience of the Single Taste," Za Paltrül Rinpoche, pp. 103–104.

REFLECTIONS ON THE POET'S OWN LIFE

"Old Dog in the Wilderness," Za Paltrül Rinpoche, pp. 417–422.

"A Song of Repentance and Disclosure," Tsangpa Gyare, pp. 228–230.

"A Long Song of Sadness," Chone Lama Rinpoche, pp. 219–223.

"Pay Heed, Pay Heed, O Zemey Tulku!" Zemey Lobsang Palden, pp. 74–75.

"A Spring Day," Kelsang Gyatso, seventh Dalai Lama, p. 409.